PASCAL PIA

Translated by Patrick Gregory

Baudelaire

Evergreen Profile Book 22

GROVE PRESS, INC. EVERGREEN BOOKS LTD.
NEW YORK LONDON

FIRST PUBLISHED IN THIS EDITION 1961. ALL RIGHTS RESERVED.

Library of Congress Catalog Card Number: 60-10251

Evergreen Profile Books are published

in the United States by Grove Press, Inc.

64 University Place   New York 3, N. Y.

in Great Britain by Evergreen Books Ltd.

20 New Bond Street   London, W. 1

First published in France by Éditions du Seuil, Paris, as Baudelaire par lui-même

MANUFACTURED BY MOUTON & CO., IN THE NETHERLANDS

Baudelaire
by Pascal Pia

Contents

Tout le bas du
visage, mauvais
pas assez d'air
le menton, pas
assez gabache

Trop de Hachures.
D'ailleurs la bouche est mauvaise,
avec quelques hachures, distribuées
Sobrement on fait le modelé.
Ceci ne doit donc être regardé
que pour la pose et l'effet
lumineux.

In 1884 a young writer by the name of Maurice Barrès wrote of the *Fleurs du Mal:* "If anyone were ever to ask my opinion, I would not hesitate to say that it is a simple book, accessible to all." In order to drive home his point, Barrès exaggerated a bit. A simple book? Well, strictly speaking, yes. Accessible to all? No. A great many people who know Baudelaire through this one work manage to find something of everything in it: charm, audacity, affectation, blasphemy – everything save simplicity. A simple book, if you insist, but simple as the confession of a poet is simple, a poet who has lived and suffered profoundly. And since this particular poet happens to be someone who was a systematic interpreter of sensations, a sensualist who, without any deliberate attempt to blacken his own character, could confess to having "cultivated his hysteria with terror and delight," the confession turns out to be truly complex, so "loaded," that its fundamental sincerity is frequently overlooked. In fact, the *Fleurs du Mal* is accessible only to those readers who have a particular predilection for Baudelaire. I think that Maurice Saillet neatly defined this poet's relationship to his public when he said that "the taste for Baudelaire requires not only some sort of initiation or indoctrination," but must also "correspond to a need, a need as profound, as irrepressible, as the need for luxury or danger. If this need does not exist," Saillet adds, "nothing will be able to bridge the gap between the reader and the work."

The very history of the *Fleurs du Mal* serves to confirm this conclusion. A great many of Baudelaire's contemporaries, and among them those who were seemingly the best suited to appreciate the book, were strangely mistaken in their judgments of its nature and importance.

5

Neither Théophile Gautier nor Sainte-Beuve – whose own verse written under the pseudonym of "Joseph Delorme" should have made him especially responsive to certain aspects of Baudelaire's poetry – was aware that this work, full of fire and fury, revealed the most sensitive, the most tormented of French poets. They doubtless noticed the startling colors of these Flowers of Evil but they were unable to perceive their perfume, their essence. Neither of them could be called a fool, and both of them certainly enjoyed the full respect of their contemporaries, yet their commentary on the *Fleurs du Mal* makes them look like country bumpkins. With all their erudition, all their undeniable talent, they had less comprehension of Baudelaire's poetry than some of the schoolboys of the period. Sainte-Beuve with his impressive mass of *Lundis*, Gautier with his countless thousands of newspaper *critiques* – the two men appeared stripped and defenseless before the *Fleurs du Mal*, and less able to cope with it than the young Swinburne, the young Mallarmé, the young Verlaine, who came to Baudelaire with empty hands but with passionate comprehension.

THAT ATROCIOUS BOOK

The scandal that surrounded the *Fleurs du Mal* at its publication in 1857, and then its later posthumous success, leaves the impression that Fate betrayed the poet. And yet, Baudelaire himself, who professed that an artist can produce nothing of value if he does not attempt to startle his readers, and who proudly proclaimed that he demanded for his works only titles that were mysterious and provocative, was partially responsible for this betrayal. But that said, it must be stated that most of his readers allowed themselves to be taken in by the bizarre and shocking aspects of the book. The notoriety of the *Fleurs du Mal* has always cast a shadow over his other important works: the *Curiosités esthétiques*, the *Art romantique*, the *Spleen de Paris*. Faced with this unjust neglect we recall the words of Shelley, a prophecy that Baudelaire delighted in quoting: "For I am one / Whom men love not, and yet regret!"

Baudelaire seems to have shared Shelley's plight. Although men profess to regret his loss, they certainly do not love him – for if they did, would they not be better acquainted with his work?

Baudelaire had contemplated writing a new preface for the second edition of the *Fleurs du Mal* in which he would attempt to dispel the "misunderstanding" that had brought about the legal condemnation of six of the book's poems. But as he set to work on this preface he was overcome by the futility of trying to explain himself to the public. In one of the drafts for this uncompleted project he wrote:

> I was imprudent enough to glance at several newspapers this morning; a sudden lassitude, the pressure of twenty atmospheres came down upon me, and I

7

collapsed under the fearful futility of attempting to explain no matter what to no matter whom. Those who really know me will grasp my meaning, and as for those who can not, or will not, understand me – any attempt at piling up explanations would be in vain.

In the draft for another preface, he once again expresses his refusal to comment on his work; the language is a blend of irony and anger:

"This book will remain as a blemish on your life," one of my friends, a great poet, predicted at the outset. Indeed, all my subsequent misfortunes have proven him right. And yet, I possess one of those felicitous characters that delights in hatred and that glories in scorn. My diabolical taste for the ridiculous permits me to take particular pleasure in the travesties of slander. Chaste as a blank sheet of paper, sober as water, prone to devotion as a young communicant, inoffensive as a born victim, it does not displease me to pass for a debauchee, a drunkard, a blasphemer and an assassin.

And certainly his "diabolical taste" was pampered by the public! Yet in spite of the general incomprehension that he met with from the very start of his career, Baudelaire never lost hope in the future of his work. On July 9, 1857, that is to say two weeks after the publication date of the *Fleurs du Mal* and before any legal action had been taken on the book, he wrote to his mother:

You know that I have always considered literature and the arts as pursuing a goal that has nothing to do with morality, and that beauty of conception and style have always been enough for me. But this book whose title, *Fleurs du Mal,* speaks for itself, is clothed, as you shall see, in a beauty that is both sinister and chilling; it has been created with fury and patience. Moreover, the proof of its positive value is in all the evil that has been spoken of it. The book makes people furious. . . .

People begrudge me everything, a creative spirit and even a knowledge of French grammar. I snap my fingers at all those imbeciles, and I know that this

volume, with all its merits and faults, will find its place in the memory of enlightened readers alongside the best poems of V. Hugo, Th. Gautier, and even Byron.

No amount of disappointment could rob Baudelaire of this conviction. Up until the very end of his life he did not cease to proclaim to his mother, to his guardian Ancelle, to his best friend Malassis: "My *Fleurs du Mal* will last." (Letter to Poulet-Malassis, May 1, 1859.)

I am convinced that the day will dawn when all that I have written will sell very well. (Letter to his mother, October 11, 1860.)

For the first time in my life I am almost content. The book (the second edition of the *Fleurs du Mal*) is almost good, and it will remain, this book, as a witness to my disgust and hatred of everything. (Letter to his mother, January 1, 1861.)

The *Fleurs du Mal....* It will begin to be understood several years from now. (Letter to Ancelle, February 18, 1866.)

It is in this letter to Ancelle, one of the last that Baudelaire was to write, that we find what is perhaps the poet's most unrestrained – and enraged – commentary on his book. He had in the past spoken to his mother of the *Fleurs du Mal* as a volume in which he had wanted "to put some of his fits of anger and melancholia" (letter of December 25, 1857). That was nothing more than an aside. In February, 1866, just before he was to find himself deprived of the ability to write and speak, he addressed a letter, or rather a proclamation to Ancelle, the anguished cry of a shattered man:

Must I explain to you, you who seem to have guessed no more than the others, that I have put my whole heart into that atrocious book, all my compassion, all my religion (travestied), all my hatred? It is true that I will write the contrary, that I will swear by all the gods that it is a work of pure art, mere monkey-play, a feat of acrobatics. And I will be lying through my teeth.

THE HAPPY DAYS

There can be no doubt that this letter of 1866 was written by a man who was very near to death. But the *Fleurs du Mal,* composed between 1841 and 1857, is already the work of someone who, if not devoured by despair, is certainly the victim of an incurable melancholia. Without attempting to present here a detailed biography of Baudelaire, it would be well to recall the fact that the death of his father in February, 1827 had, early in the poet's life, cast a shadow over his childhood. Baudelaire was at the time less than six years old. His father, François Baudelaire, who died at the age of sixty-seven, spent the last years of his life in comfortable retirement as a former administrative executive of the *Chambre des Pairs.* In 1820, a widower and already the father of a boy of fifteen, he had remarried with Caroline Dufays, a woman of twenty-seven who would undoubtedly have been condemned to a long, dull existence of respectable spinsterhood had he not appeared on the scene. These were the parents of Charles Baudelaire who was born in April 9, 1821.

It has been suggested that the disparity in age between the husband and the wife might have been partially responsible for the poet's neuropathy, his continual lack of emotional stability, and even the inarticulate stuttering of his last illness: a theory that cannot be positively refuted, but which does not seem to be entirely convincing when we consider that his half-brother, Claude Alphonse Baudelaire, also died a hemiplegic, although born of better-matched parents.

The memory of the father so soon lost to him was always to haunt the poet. During half his lifetime, and in spite of continual changes of address, he always managed to keep near him his father's portrait painted by Regnault. In the reign of Charles X, François Baudelaire still remained a figure of the eighteenth century, a faithful disciple of the *philosophes* whom he had frequently met in times gone by at Mme Helvétius' *salon* in Auteuil, and whose influence was probably instrumental in turning him away from the Church. For François Baudelaire at the age of twenty-three or twenty-four had been ordained a priest – though by the outbreak of the

MUSÉES ROYAUX
DU LOUVRE ET DU LUXEMBOURG.

CARTE D'ENTRÉE, LES JOURS D'ÉTUDE,

POUR UN ARTISTE.

Délivrée à M. *Baudelaire*

le *4 Mai* 1821

A museum pass, made out to
François Baudelaire, the poet's father.

Revolution he had abandoned his soutane. Happily employed as tutor to the children of the Duc de Choiseul-Praslin, he had refused a curacy in 1791. The arts in general, and painting in particular, had finally succeeded in wooing him away from religion. His first wife, who died in 1814, was an amateur painter, and he himself affixed his signature to several canvases which decorated walls of their little turreted house in the Rue Hautefeuille. He also compiled an album of drawings, "picture-lessons" that the old sexagenarian utilized to illustrate the rudiments of Latin which he was attempting to drum into little Charles' head.

Of what value were the paintings of François Baudelaire? Not a great deal, according to his son. But as mediocre as these paintings may have been, Charles Baudelaire had a profound sentimental attachment for them. In 1857 he was deeply moved on discovering one of them for sale at a second-hand dealer, and this discovery provoked a reproachful letter that he wrote to his mother:

> I have a disagreeable little matter to discuss with you, and I would have willingly kept it to myself if it were not that I fear that it is an indication that other errors of this sort have already been committed. A few months ago I discovered in a shop in the Passage des Panoramas one of my father's paintings (a nude figure, a reclining woman visualizing two other nude figures in her dreams). I had no money whatsoever, not even enough for a deposit, and the insufferable torrent of daily futilities caused me to neglect the affair. Do you believe that several blunders of this sort have been committed? My father was a destestable painter, but all these dusty dabblings have a moral value. (Letter of December 30, 1857.)

Apparently Caroline Dufays did not share her son's devotion to the memory of her late husband. The accepted period of mourning demanded by respectability had scarcely run its course before she became engaged, in 1828, to a dashing officer, Commander Aupick, who was only four years her senior. There can be no doubt that this hasty remarriage took the form in the troubled mind of young Charles of some sort of dark disaster, no doubt that he regarded it as a tragic betrayal. There are two poems in the *Fleurs du Mal* written in his twentieth year which reveal the vivid memories he had cherished of those first months of his mother's widowhood when the two of them lived alone together, sharing their solitude with their servant Mariette. During this summer of 1827,

13

Mme Baudelaire, in mourning since the month of February, had moved with her little son to a small country house near the Bois de Boulogne, at the border of Ternes and Neuilly.

It is this same house and this same Mariette that we find in those two early poems of the *Fleurs du Mal*. Unlike most of his other poems, Baudelaire saw fit to leave these two without titles:

I have never forgotten, so near to the city,
Our gleaming white house, small but serene,
Not its plaster Pomona and venerable Venus
Who behind a tattered hedge sheltered their nudity,
And the sun, in the evening, glistening and superb,
Dashing sheaves of light against the window-pane,
Seemed to peer in on our long and silent dinners
Like a great, astonished eye in the inquistive heavens,
Generously bestowing its last muted beams
On the frugal table-linen and the serge drapery.

*

The warm-hearted servant of whom you were so
[jealous,
Who now sleeps out her night beneath a humble plot
[of turf,
We owe her at least a few occasional flowers.
The dead, the wretched dead, have their own great
[sorrows,
And when rough October, the pruner of aged trees,
Blows his frosty winds amidst their marble slabs,
Surely they must think the living hard ungrateful
[creatures,
Tucked-up in our warm beds, while their own sad
[slumber
Is slowly devoured by shadowy reveries;
Without bed-mates, without cozy midnight conver-
[sations,
They sense the winter snows – and the passing years
Drip by their naked, worm-worked bones,
And no family, no friend, comes to replace
The faded, tattered rags that adorn the rusted grille.
If, one night when the log hisses and sings,
I should see her seated there, so calm by the fire,

If, one brittle and chill night in December,
I should come upon her, crouched in the corner of my
[chamber,
So solemn, and newly risen from her eternal bed
To give one last maternal glance at her full-grown
[child,
What could I find to say to that poor pious soul,
As I watched the tears flow from her sunken, caver-
[nous lids?

(Translated by Patrick Gregory)

In this evocation of those quiet but mournful days, this recollection of long, silent dinners, this accusation of indifference to the dead that the poet seems to be addressing to himself (but of which he was far from guilty), it would be difficult not to notice the underlying misery that his mother's behavior caused him, she who failed to share his deep attachment and who was able to spare some of her affection for her new suitor, Commander Aupick.

Many years later, in 1858, writing to his mother who had once again become a widow, Baudelaire expressed his amazement that she had never spoken to him of these two poems:

Then you have never noticed that the *Fleurs du Mal* contains two poems concerning you, or at least, which allude to certain intimate details of our past life together, to that period of your widowhood which has left me such strange and melancholy recollections? One of the poems is: "Je n'ai pas oublié, voisine de la ville . . ." (Neuilly), and the other, which follows it: "La servante au grand coeur dont vous étiez jalouse . . ." (Mariette). I left these poems without titles, without any sort of commentary, because I have a horror of prostituting intimate family things. (Letter of January 11, 1858.)

At a later date, having re-established a truly affectionate relationship with his mother, having once again found his old words of endearment, he wrote her the following lines which are both tender and heartrending:

15

Who knows whether I will one day be able to open my soul to you, this soul which you have never appreciated or understood! I write this without a moment's hesitation, for I know it to be the truth.

In my youth, there was a time when I loved you passionately – listen and read on without fear. I have never spoken to you like this before. I remember a carriage ride: you had just come out of the hospital and in order to prove to me that you had been thinking of your son during your confinement, you showed me some pen drawings that you had made for me. Do you find my memory terrifying? Later, the Place Saint-André des Arts and Neuilly. Long strolls, perpetual caresses! I remember the wharves, so very forlorn in the evenings. Ah! those were the days of my mother's tenderness for me. Excuse me for calling happy days those which were undoubtedly sad ones for you. But then you were my whole life, and you were mine alone. You were to me both idol and playmate. Perhaps you are astonished that I can speak with such passion of a time so distant. I too am astonished. It is, perhaps, because I have once again developed a longing for death that these memories of times gone by imprint themselves on my spirit. (Letter of May 6, 1861.)

MY LIFE HAS BEEN DAMNED

In fact, Baudelaire retained these memories of times gone by, and most particularly those belonging to his early childhood, in all the fresh colors of their first impression. Should we regard this obsession with the past, as he seems to suggest, as a manifestation of a death-wish? It is doubtless true that he often looked on death as the means by which to free himself from his misery. In any case, these impressions of childhood frequently served as inspiration for his poems, prose-poems, and for his *Aesthetics in the Nursery (Morale du joujou)*, which we shall have occasion to quote further on. Yet strangely enough, his memory of the first years he spent in the Aupick household seem to have been very misty. It appears that Baudelaire remembered little of this period except for the unpleasant sensation of having acquired a stepfather. There is a well-known anecdote which relates how young Charles, on the night of his mother's second marriage, locked the door of the bedroom and hurled the key out of a window: probably an apocryphal tale, but his friends heard it from his own lips, and this sardonic invention serves to sum up all that he has passed on to us concerning his life under the roof of the Aupick home.

Of his years at boarding school, first at Lyon, then at Paris, he has not said much either, but what little he has said makes it quite evident that he did not cherish a fond memory of these years. In one of his notebooks he jotted down the following autobiographical fragment: "After 1830, the Collège de Lyon, blows, fights with professors and comrades, deep fits of depression."

At eighteen, after having obtained his *bachelier* degree, the battlefield of his rebellious spirit was transferred from the classroom to the Aupick living room. His stepfather, now a general, wanted the young man to prepare for a career in the diplomatic service. Baudelaire haughtily proclaimed his intention of becoming a writer — or nothing. Recalling this domestic turmoil, Mme Aupick was to confess in 1868 to Charles Asselineau, who was then editing a posthumous collection of the poet's work:

> What a stupefying blow for us when Charles insisted on refusing all that we wanted to do for him, insisted on flying with his own wings and becoming a writer! What a sad disappointment for our household, which had up until then been so happy! What an affliction! . . .

Without realizing it, Mme Aupick underlines the auto-biographical character of the poem which, after the verses "To the Reader," opens the *Fleurs du Mal:*

BÉNÉDICTION

When from the highest power a fiat stirs
this ennuied world, the Poet suddenly
appears; his mother, frightened, in blasphemy
clenches her fists at God, who pities her:

"– Rather had I spawned a knot of vipers!
Ah, that I must suckle this derision!
Damned be that night with its ephemeral pleasures
when my womb conceived my expiation!

"Since of all women you have chosen me
to be in my husband's eyes a thing of shame,
and since I cannot throw into the flames,
like a love-letter, this dwarfed monstrosity,

"I will spew out your hate that crushes me
on this curs'd instrument of your evil mood,
and twist so well this miserable tree
that it can sprout no pestilential bud!"

Thus swallowing the white foam of her hate,
not understanding the foreplanned designs,

in deep Gehenna she rears and consecrates
funeral pyres for maternal crimes.

Guarded meanwhile by his unseen protector,
the outcast Child, drunken of sunlight, thinks
he finds again the ambrosial rosy nectar
in everything he eats, in all he drinks.

The wind's his playmate, he talks with the cloud,
exults to sing the pathway of the Rood;
and the Spirit above this pilgrim weeps aloud
to see him gay as any bird in the wood.

All those he would like to love watch him with fear,
or, growing bold from his tranquillity,
vie with each other how to draw a tear,
and test on him their own ferocity.

In the wine he drinks and even the bread he eats
they mingle obscene spittle and dusty ashes;
these hypocrites are chary of all he touches,
blaming themselves for being misled by his feet.

His woman shouts in the public square, unbridled:
"Since he finds my beauty worth his adoration,
I'll set up business as an ancient idol
and order retouched my gilded decoration;

"I'll glut myself with incense, myrrh, and nard,
with genuflexions, delicacies, and wine,
to see if, laughing, in his loving heart
I can usurp his praise of the divine.

"And when I weary of this impious farce,
my delicate and clever hands will start
with their strong nails, like harpies' claws, to force
a little highway even to his heart.

"Like a young bird trembling in its nest,
like a tidbit to sate my favorite hound,
I'll tear his heart all bloody from his breast
and cast it with disdain upon the ground!"

The Poet lifts his pious arms, serene,
toward the sky where shines a throne of light,
and the vast lightnings of his spirit screen
the raging of the rabble from his sight:

"Praise be God who bade that we endure
pain's holy balm for our impurities,
most potent of elixirs and most pure,
which steels the strong with holy ecstacies!

"I know you keep a place among the blest
and happy Legions, as the Poet's own,
where he is bidden to the eternal feast
with the Dominions, Virtues, and the Thrones;

"I know that grief's unique nobility
is something earth and hell cannot destroy,
that time and all the worlds are forced for me
to weave a mystic coronal of joy.

"But neither unknown metals nor lost gems
of old Palmyra, nor pearls from the sea,
though mounted by your hands, suffice for me
as does this lucent glittering diadem;

"For it shall be of nothing but pure light
from the holy hearth of primal rays, and clearer
than any mortal eyes, however bright,
which are no more than dismal obscure mirrors!"
                              (Translated by C. F. MacIntyre)

There is no mistaking the fact; in this ill-starred
poet, idealized as he may be, Baudelaire forces us to
acknowledge his own image. The very place that he re-
serves for him, at the threshold of his book, indicates that
it is this same poet who is about to utter his confession
in the *Fleurs du Mal*. In Baudelaire's opinion, the Poet,
the anonymous poet, is not necessarily doomed to dam-
nation. In a letter of January 21, 1856 he wrote to
Alphonse Toussenel: "For a long time I have been
maintaining that the poet is *supremely* intelligent,
that he is the epitome of *intelligence*." Intelligence
is not automatically linked to misery. Banville certainly
cannot be regarded as an "accursed poet" and it is to his
work that Baudelaire is referring when he says that
"poetry represents the beautiful hours of one's existence,
that is to say, the hours when one feels happy to think,
to be alive." The malediction that he denounces in the
poem "Bénédiction" he looks upon as a denial of per-

sonal justice, an arbitrary sentence handed down without appeal. He speaks of this to his mother:

> I believe that my life has been damned from the very beginning and that it is damned for eternity. (Letter of December 4, 1854.)

BAUDELAIRE AT THE AGE OF TWENTY

At the time that Baudelaire wrote those words he was thirty-three years of age. When did he first become convinced that he was doomed to live out a tragedy? I we refer to the first pages of his journals, we could assume that he held this belief since adolescence. In reality, this profound pessimism – though he first sensed its presence at the age of six when he lost his father – did not actually take possession of him until he was twenty, and even then he refused to acknowledge his affliction. His "lively appetite for life and pleasure" that Baudelaire recalls in *My Heart Laid Bare (Mon coeur mis à nu)*, induced him to adopt, on leaving school, a mode of existence that shocked and alarmed his family. He haphazardly divided his time between libraries, museums, literary acquaintances, and prostitutes. His courtship of Balzac and de Nerval disturbed the Aupicks no less than his midnights revels in the company of streetwalkers. In order to tear the young man away from this intellectual and sensual debauchery, a family council was convened. It was decreed that he and Paris were to be separated from one another for several months. On June 9, 1841, Baudelaire embarked from Bordeaux on the liner *Paquebot-des-Mers-du-Sud* which was to carry him as far as the Isle of Réunion, where, slipping away from the captain to whose care he had been entrusted, he re-embarked in the month of October and returned to Paris in 1842 after having visited (or so he let it be known) Colombo and Calcutta.

It is the memories brought back from this unsolicited "vacation" that are responsible for several poems in the *Fleurs du Mal* distinguishable by their exoticism ("La Vie Antérieure," "Parfum exotique," "A une Dame créole," "Bien loin d'ici," "A une Malabaraise"), and for numerous scattered images evoking the sea.

Banville, reporting some of the conversations he had had with Baudelaire, relates that "in some African country," the poet, "lodging with friends of his family, soon became exasperated by the banality of his hosts' household and went off to live alone on a mountain top, accompanied by a very young and very tall native girl who knew no French and who cooked up strangely spiced stews in an enormous polished copper cauldron around which naked little Negro children danced and shouted. Ah! those stews, how well he described them, how he roused our appetites!" Baudelaire did not always scorn to embellish the truth in order to beguile his friends. Nonetheless, it is true that while staying at the Isle of Maurice, at the home of a M. Autard de Bragard, he made the acquaintance of a young native girl from

Malabar, the stepsister of his host's wife. It was for Mme Autard de Bragard that he wrote the sonnet "A une Dame Créole," composed on the Isle of Réunion in 1841 and which found its way into the first edition of the *Fleurs du Mal* though little more than a *pièce de circonstance*, a pleasingly turned compliment. Less successful as a poem, weighted down with verbiage and frequently marred by what Baudelaire calls his "infantile style," his "A une Malabaraise" (which was admitted into the *Fleurs du Mal* only after the poet's death) is nevertheless of interest to his biographers:

A UNE MALABARAISE

Your feet are delicate as your hands, your heavy
haunch would fill the lovliest white with envy;
to the thoughtful artist your body is sweet and fresh;
your velvet eyes are browner than your flesh.

Born beneath hot blue skies, your only tasks
are to keep cool water and perfume in the flasks,
to light your master's pipe and chase away
mosquitoes from his bed; when the new day
makes plane-trees sing, already you are
buying pineapples and bananas in the bazaar.
All day, here and there, on naked feet
you wander as you wish and hum those sweet
outlandish songs. On scarlet-mantled eves
you stretch your body on soft mats of leaves,
in drifting dreams where hummingbirds dart through
a landscape gracious, flowery as you.

Happy child, why wish you to see our France,
its too many people mowed down by mischance,
and bidding good-bye to your dear tamarinds,
trust your life to lusty sailors and rough winds?
There, half-dressed in muslins, you would go
shivering through the brunt of hail and snow.
How you'd regret your happy carefree pranks
when brutal corsets prison your soft flanks!
when you must glean your supper from our mud
by selling the fragrance of your exotic blood.

23

Through our dirty fog you would follow with sad eyes
a mirage of cocoa palms from absent skies.

(Translated by C. F. MacIntyre)

Distance did not efface the image of this Malabar girl.
Nor did time. We meet her again in two other works
of Baudelaire which date from a much later period: the
inverted sonnet entitled "Bien loin d'ici" and the prose-
poem "La Belle Dorothée" where she appears with all
her charms:

> She advances, softly balancing her slender waist on
> her ample thighs. Her robe of clinging silk, bright and
> rose colored, forms a vivid contrast with her shadowy
> skin and brings into play the sharp outlines of her
> long waist, the hollows in her back, and her pointed
> breasts.
>
> Her red umbrella, filtering the light, tints her face
> with the blood-colored rouge of its reflections.
>
> The weight of her luxuriant blue-black hair pulls back
> her delicately shaped head and gives her a triumphant
> and idle air. Her heavy ear-rings twitter confidentially
> behind her tiny ears.
>
> From time to time sea breeze lifts by a corner her
> floating skirt and reveals her superb, gleaming legs;
> and her feet, like the feet of marble goddesses that
> Europe emprisons in its museums, faithfully imprint
> their form in the fine sand. For Dorothée is so pro-
> digiously coquettish, that the pleasure of being admired
> excites her more than the pride of being a free woman,
> and, although she is free, she walks without shoes.

If we see here a faithful portrait of Dorothée, we can
suppose that the memory of this exotic native girl played
an important part in developing Baudelaire's obsession
for a certain type of feminine beauty. The traits that he
attributes to Dorothée are not very different than those
which, shortly after his return to Paris in 1842, he was
to find so irresistible in the person of Jeanne Duval. But
we will later have occasion to speak of this mulatto
woman who, as is well known, was the only mistress
with whom Baudelaire was to form a lasting attachment.

SAMUEL CRAMER AT THE DINNER TABLE

Shortly after his return from the Isle of Réunion, Baudelaire attained his majority. New literary friendships occupied his time, for this was the period when he made the acquaintance of Théophile Gautier, who was ten years older than he, and Théodore de Banville, two years his junior. And now he could claim from his family the inheritance left him by his father which amounted to some hundred thousand francs, that is to say, about twenty million 1952 francs. A considerable sum in those days when large-scale industrialism had not yet awakened and developed the needs and temptations of the twentieth-century man.

Knowing Baudelaire's characteristic prodigality, the Aupick household constantly withheld payment of his funds. The young heir, who was already deep in debt, sank yet deeper. Dandyism, as he intended to practice it, was very expensive, for he demanded – in everything – nothing less than perfection. Baudelaire the Dandy wore only clothes tailored to his own very special specifications: a blue coat with metal buttons, that he had remarked in a portrait of Goethe; a short black jacket with tails that flaired out in the back; a velvet vest that seemed molded to his body; billowing cashmere trousers which defied the tight-fitting mode of the day. The books that particularly caught his fancy he had bound in morocco leather by the best binders of Paris. The same craving for distinction dictated the adornment of his table; a dandy could not help but be a gourmet, as is Samuel Cramer, Fanfarlo's lover and Baudelaire's half-wistful, half-whimsical caricature of himself:

Samuel and Fanfarlo had precisely the same views on cooking, and on the sort of nourishment necessary to sustain the "chosen few." Banal meat and insipid fishes were rigorously excluded from these sylph-like suppers. Champagne rarely dishonored his table. The most renowned, the most delicately perfumed Bordeaux gave way to a formidable, tight-ranked battalion of Burgundies, and then trooped in wines from Auvergne, Anjou, the Midi, and foreign wines from Germany, Greece, and Spain. Samuel used to declare that a true glass of wine should resemble a cluster of black grapes and that there should be in the glass as much to eat as to drink. - Fanfarlo loved meats that bled and wines that brought intoxication at a gallop. - And yet, she was never drunk. - Both of them professed a profound esteem for the truffle. - The truffle, that mute and mysterious plant of Cybele, that delectable malady that she keeps hidden in her womb longer than the most precious metals, that exquisite substance that defies the agronomist's science, as gold defied that of Paracelsus; the truffle, that common glory of both the ancient and the modern world, and which, before a glass of *chic*, has the effect of a string of zeros after a number.

As for the question of sauces, ragoûts, and spices (a grave question which would demand a chapter as sober and serious as could be found in any scientific text-book), I can assure you that they were both in complete accord, especially on the necessity of enlisting the aid of all Nature's pharmaceutical stock in the kitchen. Pimentos, English powders, sassafras, colonial importations, concoctions from the Orient, everything seemed to find a suitable role, especially musk and incense. If Cleopatra were alive today, I am certain that she would choose to garnish her cuts of beef or venison with Arabian perfumes. Surely it is deplorable that the *cordons bleus* of today are not compelled by some particular voluptuary law to learn the chemical properties of substances so that they should be able to discover, for the necessary occasions - such as a lovers' banquet, for example - certain almost inflammable culinary elements, prompt to penetrate the organic system, like prussic acid, and to evaporate like ether.

Without any doubt - and let us repeat this point -

Baudelaire presents Samuel Cramer as a highly exaggerated caricature of himself: the poet, as we know, never claimed the honor of being a new Apicius. However, he has Cramer profess, in his pursuit of culinary delight, an Epicurianism that no dandy would dare disavow.

Banville has described the eloquence Baudelaire could find to lavish on the ragoûts of his Malabar mistress. And, in his correspondence, we sometimes surprise the poet dispensing culinary advice to his friends. For de Vigny, who suffered from a rebellious digestive system, he prescribes the produce of one of the best pastry kitchens of Paris:

> One of my friends has told me that Guerre, the English pastry cook who has an establishment at the corner of the rue Castiglione and the rue de Rivoli, makes some meat patés blended with very hot wine, Madeira or Xérès no doubt, that even the most miserable stomachs can digest with ease and pleasure! It is a sort of wine and meat jelly more substantial, more nourishing, than a complete menu. (Letter of February, 1862.)

De Vigny also received some advice from Baudelaire on the choosing of his beer:

> One is so easily enchanted by your presence, Monsieur, that I neglected to speak to you yesterday on the subject of good and evil ales. Since you wish to experiment with a diet, let me warn you to avoid like the plague (and I'm not exaggerating; it has made me ill in the past) any bottle carrying the trade-mark Harris. That man is a pernicious poisoner.
>
> Although Allsopp and Bass are good names (Bass especially) it is best to be suspicious of their labels as well, because of counterfeit producers. The safest thing for you to do is to procure your ale from one of the two reputable addresses that I am going to give you and where you can trade with confidence. (Undated letter, end of January, 1862.)

We find him offering some gingerbread to Sainte-

fund.... Samuel ... — a ... after ... in ... but we ... obtained the ... and Antaeus. However, he ... Croce-... much of ... Byron ... and their theory.

Darwin... the... other authors. And in his ... the ... requires the poet ... De Vigny, ... Chénier, Diderot, be ... spoke of the ... Latinism in ...

One ... has ... that Courbet, the [?] ... the ... in the ... of ... in the ... rue de Rivoli, ... court ... for the ... Delacroix, ... was abnormal. It has ... man [?] more ... that ... he ... the great distorter, Edgar ... the ... one ... upon ... Shorthor[?] of his ...

BAUDELAIRE, BY MANET (1862)

Beuve, along with a brief commentary on that intriguing topic:

> A few days ago, sensing a sudden need for your company – just as Antaeus had need of the Earth – I made my way to the rue Montparnasse. On the way I passed by a gingerbread baker and the idea came to me that you must certainly be a devotee of ginger-bread. Remember that nothing is better in wine, at dessert; and I felt sure that I was going to drop by your place just as you were finishing your dinner. I hope that you have not taken that piece of ginger-bread, incrusted with angelica, as some sort of knavish joke, and that you have eaten it without ceremony.
>
> If you share my taste, I recommend – when you can find it – English gingerbread, very thick, very black, so dense that there are neither holes nor pores, and packed full of anis and ginger. It should be cut in slices as thin as roastbeef, and can be spread with butter or jam. (Letter of July 1, 1860.)

FIRST HUMILIATIONS

But this gingerbread is the gift of an impoverished Baudelaire. In 1842 he felt himself rich. And consequently he regaled his friends in magnificent style. He opened his purse to them, and the money-lenders willingly replenished it when he had run through the monthly allotment doled out by his parents. The Aupicks, fearing his extravagance, were eager to prevent him from putting his hands on the capital of his inheritance. Nadar, who knew Baudelaire in these early days, used to recall the poet's generosity with a smile of pleasure: "Baudelaire at twenty," he said, "lived according to the motto of Ravenswood: 'The Open Hand.'"

This prodigality was evidently displayed out of sight of the Aupick household. In June, 1842 he moved into an apartment building on the Ile Saint-Louis, 10 Quai de Béthune (today number 22), where he rented a single room, vast and high-ceilinged, on the ground floor. He remained there only a few months at most. In April, 1843 he inhabited another ground-floor flat, on the rue Vaneau, and in October of that year he returned once again to the Ile Saint-Louis where he set up house at 17 Quai d'Anjou in one of the flats of the Pimodan mansion, formerly the residence of Lauzun, which had recently become the property of the Baron Jérôme Pichon. Three domiciles in sixteen months, and there were doubtless others as well, for our biograhphical material on this period of his life is not without many gaps. Baudelaire's bohemianism prevented him from settling down anywhere. He has remarked upon this trait of his in *My Heart Laid Bare* with the intention of analyzing its causes at some later date:

A study of that grave illness: a horror of having a

29

permanent address. Reasons for the illness. Progressive growth of the illness.

But Baudelaire was never to write this analysis, for he changed literary projects as often as he changed addresses. In his life as in his work, he was a vagabond, the victim of his own restless personality. The art of making a career, of "establishing himself," was wholly foreign to his nature. Even when reason and self-interest urged him to take a definite course of action, and to hold firm to it, he instinctively rebelled. He could not help but feel that all decisive gestures were a sort of condemnation, a prelude to death.

We can not be at all certain as to the extent of Baudelaire's literary activity during these years of his youth. It is known that in 1843 he collaborated with Prarond, a young writer of his own age, in the composition of a never-to-be-completed drama in verse entitled *Idéolus*, and that he offered several satirical articles, which were too audacious for publication, to such periodicals as the *Tintamarre* and the *Démocratie pacifique*. He also lent a hand in the writing of an anonymous publication called *Mystères galans des théâtres de Paris*, a potpourri of behind-the-scenes scandals and malicious gossip, which earned him the enmity of one of his creditors, the art-dealer Arondel, and of his aristocrat landlord, the Baron Pichon.

But these were nothing but mere scribblings to which he attached little importance. What he took to heart was his poetry, and this he had not yet submitted to any newspapers or reviews. By the end of 1843 he had already written about fifteen of the poems which were later to appear in the *Fleurs du Mal*. At the moment he was content to read them aloud to his close friends and then lay them aside while the bold structure of his future work slowly took form in his mind. He contemplated a collection of poems which would, as he said, "launch him into posterity like a cannon ball."

In the meantime money flowed through his fingers, and at such a rate that his parents began to fear that his inheritance would soon be entirely dissipated. He dreamed of supplementing his income by dashing off a few novels and, during the first monhts of 1844, wrote his mother what he hoped would be a reassuring letter:

> I assure you that when I have scribbled off two or three novels, I shall have no trouble at all in getting them published. Two months of work should be sufficient. A novel of ten good-sized chapters is worth – on the average – five hundred francs, a novel of ten installments for a review, one thousand.

The sum was of little importance for he was to die without ever having completed a novel, and probably, without ever having written the first chapter of that *Homme aux Ruysdaels* which, in 1846, was announced for imminent publication by a Paris newspaper. In fact, as far as fiction was concerned, Baudelaire found it impossible to go beyond the short story, and even in that form he was noticeably ill at ease. His genius was not that of a maker of plots or a creator of characters. Indeed, it would be difficult to imagine a more subjective writer than Baudelaire. If he spent so much devoted labor on his translations of Poe, it was only because he found something of himself in the work and personality of the American poet. And if, among all the painters who captured his enthusiasm, Constantin Guys was the one he served best, the reason can perhaps be found in the curious spiritual and aesthetic ties that linked the two men: Baudelaire's own drawings could almost be mistaken for rough sketches by Guys, and the subject matter of many of Guys' canvases almost seem to have been dictated by Baudelaire's imagination.

However that may be, Baudelaire's efforts as a novelist did nothing to alleviate his financial distress. His family, genuinely horrified by his continued extravagance, made frantic attempts to keep him from squandering the remaining portion of his patrimony. Their vigilance only caused him to lose his temper. He wrote his mother:

> It seems to me that you have acted in extremely bad taste in sending that friend of yours (or was it a disguised lackey?) around to my restaurant in order to persuade the proprietor to discontinue my credit.

31

Spare me this nursemaiding. . . . (Letter of March 3, 1844.)

But the "nursemaiding" was to become ever more restrictive. The Aupicks finally decided to resort to legal action and to put their son's estate in the hands of an administrator, a lawyer from Neuilly by the name of Ancelle. In a letter meant for her eyes alone, Baudelaire pleads with his mother to renounce this drastic measure; he would agree to submit his expenses to maternal supervision, but the introduction of a third party into his affairs would be an unbearable humiliation for him:

I beseech you to read this letter with the greatest attention because it is a very serious one, it is a final appeal to your good sense and to the profound affection that you claim to have for me. First of all I send you this under the seal of secrecy and implore you to show it to no one.

Secondly, I beg you on bended knees to see in this no intention to provoke pathos, or to touch you in any way save through sound reasoning. The curious manner in which all our discussion seem to turn into bitter carping (though there is seldom any real anger on my part), the agitated state in which I now find myself, your deliberate refusal to listen to anything that I have to say, all this has forced me to resort to a pen in order to persuade you how much you are now in the wrong in spite of your affection for me.

I write all this with a cool head after having thought out the whole matter with the greatest care, and when I consider the sickness that has gripped me for the last few days, brought on by anger and bewilderment, I can not help but wonder how I shall ever be able to endure what has happened! You keep repeating, in order to make me swallow the pill, that there is nothing abnormal, nothing dishonorable in all this. That may be, I'm willing to believe you; but to speak the truth, what do I care how other people may regard the matter if I feel so entirely different about it? You tell me that my anger and grief will pass away with time, you presume that treating me like a bawling baby you are doing me a service. But do try to make yourself understand – and you seem to be totally unaware of this fact – that, unhappily for me, I am not made like other men. What you regard as simply a necessary and regrettable course of action, is to me something unbearable, absolutely unbearable. That's clear enough. You can, when we are alone, treat me in whatever fashion you please, but I will fight tooth and nail against any attempt to restrict my freedom. Isn't it an act of incredible cruelty to subject me to the intervention of men who find this whole affair of mine very tiresome and who don't even know me personally? And, between the two of us, who can boast of really knowing me, of knowing what I want to do, where I want to go, how much I can put up with without losing all patience? I sincerely believe that you have made a grave mistake. I say so coolly, for I look upon myself as already condemned by you, and I am certain that you will not listen to me. But pay attention to this: you have caused me, knowingly and willfully, infinite pain, of which you are incapable of guessing the intensity. (Undated letter, 1844.).

These entreaties were to be in vain. In the month of September, 1844, Baudelaire's inheritance was placed in the care of the lawyer Ancelle who, though certainly a scrupulous and devoted administrator, was as little able as Mme Aupick to appreciate the poet's personality and to cope with his over-sensitive nature. To have his income doled out to him by an attorney – as though he were a minor or a lunatic – was to submit Baudelaire, on his début in the world of letters, to a terrible humiliation. And as he grew older, this sense of humiliation only grew deeper, more unbearable. To make matters worse, another misfortune overtook him at this period – the first signs of syphilis. Although the first symptoms soon disappeared, the disease was never to lose its hold on him. Utterly frustrated by his mother's lack of confidence in him, permanently scarred by his first contacts with physical love – these two early setbacks could not fail to have a great effect on one whose life depended so much on women.

Drawing by Baudelaire, bearing the notation:
"Sample sketch for Antique Beauty, *dedicated to Chenavard."*

THE FRAGRANCE OF WOMEN

In a confidential aside, Baudelaire wrote to Sainte-Beuve:

> One day, in some wretched newspaper, I came across several lines referring to my repulsive ugliness, certainly written so as to make me out an utterly unattractive individual. (A cruel blow for a man who has always loved the fragrance of women as much as I.) (Letter of January, 1862.)

There are few works of Baudelaire which are not impregnated with this fragrance. One senses it in his poetry, in his prose-poems, in his *Fanfarlo,* in his essay *The Painter and Modern Life.* Among the four little boys who figure in his prose-poem *Les Vocations,* each of them exhibiting a distinctive trait of the poet's character, there is one who has already succumbed to the intoxication of the feminine presence:

> "Listen, I'm going to tell you about something that I did, something that I'll bet none of you has ever done. . . . A few days ago my parents took me with them on a trip and, when we stopped at an inn for the night, there weren't enough beds for all of us so I had to sleep with our maid." He drew his playmates around him, and lowered his voice. "I'm telling you, it's an odd sort of feeling not to be all alone in bed, and to be lying there with the maid right beside you like that, and the darkness all around. I couldn't get to sleep, and while she slept I ran my hand along her arm, and her neck, and her breasts too. She's built bigger than any other woman in the world, and her skin is so soft, so very, very soft, that you'd think it was fancy letter-paper, or that paper made out of silk.

It was so nice that I could have kept it up most of the night if I only wasn't scared; scared of awakening her, and scared of ... well, I don't know what. Then I nestled my head in her hair which hangs all the way down her back, as thick as a lion's mane, and it smelled as good – honest! – as the flowers right here in the garden. Go ahead and try it sometime – if you ever get the chance – and see whether I'm telling you the truth!"

The young author of this fabulous revelation narrated his adventure with wondering, glowing eyes, still stupefied by the recollection of his experience, and the rays of the setting sun, shimmering in his tousled hair, seemed to ignite a sulfurous halo of passion amidst his russet curls.

A laconic note in his journals recalls a very young Baudelaire who was no less sensitive to feminine fragrances than the ardent little urchin of *Les Vocations*:

Precocious taste for women. I used to confuse the odor of their furs with the odor of the women themselves. I remember. ... In brief, I loved my mother for her elegance. I was thus a precocious dandy. (From *Fusées*.)

For a sensualist like Baudelaire, there were no sensations that did not serve to arouse his appetite for the world of women. In the *Fleurs du Mal* we even find him exploring the underworld of Lesbian love. A voice can bewitch him, a flowing mass of hair intoxicates him with its fragrance. This sexual dandyism evidently requires a sort of refinement akin to that of the gourmet, and which is, according to Baudelaire, one of the characteristics of a true artist: that refinement, for example, that he recognized in Thomas de Quincey whose childhood was hemmed in by women. Baudelaire comments on this in his *Paradis artificiels*:

The man who from the very beginning of his life has been bathed in the soft atmosphere of women, in the odor of their hands, their breasts, their limbs, their hair, their supple, flowing garments,

36

une femme
pour Asselineau

DRAWING BY BAUDELAIRE

La Fanfarlo —

La Fanfarlo, as sketched by Baudelaire.
At right: her lover, Samuel Cramer
— Baudelaire himself.

Dulce balneum suavibus
Unguentatum odoribus,

has acquired from this society a delicacy of touch, a
refinement of accent, a sort of androgyny, without
which the heartiest, the most virile genius remains, as
far as perfection of his art is concerned, an incom-
plete being. In short, I mean that a precocious taste
for the world of women, *mundi muliebris*, for all its
undulating appurtenances, its glimmer and its perfume,
gives birth to the superior geniuses.

In the above passage we find the charm of the woman
blended and confused with the charm of her garments,
the attraction of the mistress with the attraction of her
toilette. Like Mallarmé, (one of his spiritual heirs),
Baudelaire would perhaps have found it fascinating to
edit a fashion magazine. In his essay on Guys, *The
Painter and Modern Life,* he lovingly describes the
muslins and gauzes, the caressing clouds of cloth which
are "the attributes and the pedestal" of the feminine
divinity:

Where is the man who, in the street, at the theatre,
in the park, has never contemplated with delight, in an
entirely disinterested manner, a knowingly composed
toilette, and has not carried away with him a confused
image of feminine beauty, making of the two, the
woman and the grown, an indivisible totality?

There are frequent allusions to gowns and jewels in the
Fleurs du Mal, and they are usually found in the most
torrid passages:

My darling was naked, but knowing my tastes
Had carefully kept on her sonorous jewels . . .
(Les Bijoux)

From her thick and supple head of hair,
That breathing sachet, that censor of love,
A scent ascended, musky and wild,

And from her velvet and muslin robes,
So deeply imbued with her pure maidenhood,
There crept the savage perfume of furs.
(Un Fantôme: le Parfum)

La Fanfarlo, which dates from 1846 at the latest, already reveals Baudelaire's fascination for the whole "world of women," for elaborate dresses and sophisticated cosmetics. Samuel Cramer, Fanfarlo's lover, adores "rouge and ceruse, pinchbeck and all sorts of back-stage embellishments. He would gladly have repainted the trees and the sky, and if God had seen fit to appoint him as His chief decorator, Cramer would have perhaps succeeded in botching-up the whole of Nature."

Cramer certainly bears a great resemblance to his author. In a little notebook that did double duty as both an address book and an account book, and which seems to belong to the period between 1861 and 1863, that is to say, some fifteen years after *La Fanfarlo*, one can read Baudelaire's detailed observations on the toilette of a certain Agathe, a woman whose identity has never been discovered:

AGATHE.

Little girl's hairdo, curled and flowing down her back.

Facial make-up. Eyebrows, lashes, lips. Some rouge, powder, beauty marks.

Earrings, necklaces, bracelets, rings.

Low-cut gown, bare arms. No crinoline.

Stockings of very fine silk, latest mode, black if the gown is black or brown. Rose if the gown is light colored. Very open shoes. Gay garters.

A bath. Feet and hands carefully cared for. Carefully scented.

Because of hairdo, when going to the dance, be covered, if we go.

"If we go ..." Ah, that makes us pause a moment! Yes, we can picture the poet with Agathe leaning lightly on his arm, as bright and as elegant as one of Guys' little coquettes. Perhaps it was to Agathe that he addressed the lines of *Moesta et errabunda*:

That innocent paradise, full of furtive pleasures,
Is it – so soon – more remote than India or China?

PROSTITUTE OR HOUSEKEEPER?

This man who was so obsessed by women – what sort of women did he choose to make, or dream to make, his mistresses and friends? In his *Advice to Young Writers (Conseils aux jeunes littérateurs)*, written when he was himself a young writer of twenty-five, he states that women "are dangerous for men of letters," and proceeds to expound several aphorisms where the paradoxical, or ironical, tone should not blind us to the underlying sincerity of his convictions:

> If I want to keep faith with the law of contrasts that governs the moral and physical order of our universe, I am obliged to include in my classification of women that are dangerous for men of letters the "virtuous wife," the blue-stocking, and the actress: the "virtuous wife," because she necessarily belongs to two men and thus provides poor pasture for the despotic soul of a poet; the blue-stocking, because she is simply an unsuccessful imitation of a man; the actress, because she is all decked out in literature, and speaks the language of the street – in short, because she is not a woman in the true sense of the word, her public being more precious to her than any lover.
>
> Can you imagine a poet who is in love with his wife allowing her to play a travesty of herself on the stage? It seems to me that he would end by setting fire to the theatre.
>
> Can you imagine his being obliged to write a role for a wife who has no talent?
>
> And our poet sweating to find the proper phrases that would put across to the public the misery that it has caused him through the creature that he loves most in the world – a creature that an Oriental potentate would shut away in the innermost recesses of his harem, before coming to Paris to study law? Because

all true writers have, at certain moments, a horror of literature, it seems to me that there are to suit their needs – the needs of spirits that are free and proud, tired spirits that seek repose on the seventh day – only two acceptable types of women: prostitutes or imbeciles, love or "domestic bliss." Brothers, need I bother to explain my reasons?

That the poet had to choose between the prostitute and the housekeeper was a conviction that Baudelaire never relinquished. In 1852 he returned to this subject in an essay on Poe in which he said of women that "their stunted education, their political and literary incompetence, prevent many writers from regarding them as anything but household utensils or objects of lust."

In one of his notebooks, published later under the title of *My Heart Laid Bare*, we find him pondering over the following question: "Why the man of intellect prefers prostitutes to society women, although both of them are equally stupid? – Point to be examined more closely."

But it is quite clear that he refers here only to partners in pleasure and not to true companions. Perhaps he has found a partial answer to his question when he adds just a few lines later:

> There are some women who resemble the ribbon of the *Légion d'honneur*. One wants nothing more to do with them because they have been soiled by certain men.
>
> And for the same reason, I would never borrow the trousers of a flea-bitten tramp.

This explanation, however, is obviously conditioned by Baudelaire's own bitterness and despair; and if he haunted the dingy brothels of Paris during the sixties, it was only because of the illness that he contracted in his youth.

Nonetheless, we know for a fact – his correspondence with his mother and his friends provides ample evidence – that Baudelaire had one, and only one, true and lasting love affair. It dated from his twentieth year when he fell in love with a young mulatto woman (or was she a quadroon?) who played bit-parts in a small Paris theatre.

JEANNE DUVAL

The biography of Jeanne Duval is yet to be written.
It is thought that her real name was Jeanne Lemer, but
even this basic fact remains uncertain, for in order to
elude her creditors she changed her name several times;
and in 1864 we meet her as Mlle Prosper. But if her
true identity is something of a mystery, her physical
appearance is well known to us, thanks to the pen
drawings Baudelaire made of her, to his many allusions
to her in his poems, and to the reminiscences of the poet's
friends.

Jeanne Duval could be readily recognized by her
triumphant walk which, according to Banville, had something both divine and bestial about it; by her startlingly
black hair – almost blue in its blackness – with flowing
curls; by her very large brown eyes, her sensual lips, and,
to borrow one of Baudelaire's own terms, her "sharp
neck" which, judging from the *Fleurs du Mal*, held a
particular fascination for the poet.

As for her character, what we know of it certainly
seems to indicate that she was not made for domestic
tranquility. Jeanne Duval displayed all the evil traits
that are traditionally attributed to persons of mixed racial
parentage. Artful, lying, debauched, extravagant, alco-
holic, and, in addition, stupid and illiterate, she would
perhaps have been more at home in the world of prostitutes than in the company of artists. Baudelaire most
assuredly had her in mind when he declared, somewhat
gratuitously, in an article entitled "Les Drames et les
romans honnêtes" (1851), that "generally speaking, the
mistresses of poets are ugly sluts of whom the least bad
of the lot are those who know how to cook up a decent
soup and who do not turn over their money to another
lover."

Caricature of Jeanne Duval, by Baudelaire

But whatever Jeanne's faults may have been, whatever her vices and infidelities, it must be stated in her defense that the sort of life she led with Baudelaire was not designed to raise her out of. her moral and physical depravity. Baudelaire was well aware of this fact and could never supress a feeling of guilt concerning her.

In the course of this sordid romance, constantly shattered by quarrels and hastily patched up again, the poet had a thousand occasions to curse the stupidity of his mistress. But then, had he not himself recommended young writers to choose stupid mistresses? A victim of his own principles, did he pick Jeanne for her lack of brains as well as for her abundance of physical attractions? In his "Choix de Maximes consolantes sur l'amour," published in the *Corsaire-Satan* of March, 1846, we find the following lines that perhaps reflect his own image of Jeanne:

There are some men who blush for having loved a woman as soon as they become aware that she is a stupid fool. Such men are conceited asses, fit only to nibble on the favors of wicked old hags or blue-stockings. Stupidity is often the adornment of beauty; it is what gives a woman's eyes that mournful limpidity of dark pools, that oily tranquility of tropical seas. Stupidity is often the preservative of beauty; it repells wrinkles; it is a divine cosmetic that keeps our idols safe from the ravages of the intellect that so disfigure us, wretched pedants that we are!"

Unfortunately, Jeanne's restful stupidity was wedded to a moral depravity that caused her lover untold misery. He is doubtless drawing from his own sad experience when, in his "Choix de maximes consolantes," he speaks of the conflict between the spirit and the senses:

I could write on for many more pages if I wished to enumerate all the beautiful and noble aspects of what people choose to call vice and moral ugliness; but for men of heart and intellect there often arises a difficult and agonizing predicament that touches on tragedy when they find themselves caught between an hereditary and habitual taste for morality and the tyrannical influence of a woman who deserves nothing but scorn. Her numerous and sordid infidelities, her whorish ways, those shameful secrets that reveal themselves to you against your will, make you loathe the creature, and it sometimes happens that your very pleasure causes you to shudder with horror. And there you are, bogged down in your Platonic reasonings. Virtue and pride cry out: Flee her! But nature whispers: Flee where? Fearful alternatives where the best fortified spirits reveal the insufficiency of their philosophic education. The cleverest men, finding themselves forced by nature into acting out the eternal dramas of Manon Lescaut and Leone Leoni, overcome their scruples by declaring that love and scorn invariably go hand in hand.

This conclusion of the "cleverest men" seems to have been adopted by Baudelaire himself. In the poem "Femmes damnées," one of the pieces of the *Fleurs du Mal* that he was still revising on the proof-sheets just a few days before the book went to press, did he not firmly maintain that love and morality are incompatible?

> That idle dreamer be eternally accursed
> Who first, through his stupidity involved
> In a fruitless problem that cannot be solved,
> Confused matters of love with probity!
>
> He who would unite in mystic bond,
> Gloom and glow, day and night,
> Will never warm his numbed body in the light
> Of this red sun that's known as love.
>
> (Translated by Helen R. Lane)

For Baudelaire, whose lapses from faith never freed him from a terrible awareness of sin, the flesh was always identified with Evil; for him, love and duty were antitheses. When a man thus divorces pleasure and conscience it is not surprising that all his brief moments of voluptuousness should leave him with a bitter aftertaste:

> What is so very annoying about love is that it is a crime that can not be committed without an accomplice. (*My Heart Laid Bare*)

46

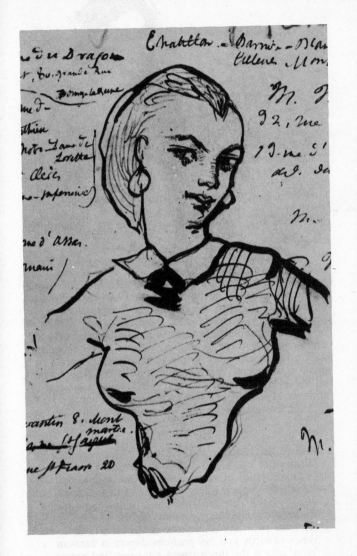

JEANNE DUVAL
Drawing by Baudelaire.

JEANNE DUVAL
*Pen-and-ink drawing.
dated (in Poulet-Ma-
lassis' hand)
February 27, 1865.*

The nature of his relationship with Jeanne, and the sort of pleasures that this relationship afforded him, only served to increase his initial uneasiness. Between his mistress and himself there could be no possible communion save in bed. He is far from the "green paradise of juvenile passions." Indeed, he has brought himself to the Subur, and there he lingers. Jeanne Duval occupies such a prominent place in the *Fleurs du Mal,* haunts so many of the poems, that it would be difficult to reproduce all the texts pertaining to her in this little volume. Here, however, are three poems which are certainly impregnated with the presence of his dark-skinned muse:

SED NON SATIATA

Bizarre deity, dusky as the night,
Scenting of musk and leaves of Havana,
Midnight labor of some Faust of the savanna,
My ebony-thighed witch, daughter of the shadows,

Rather than constancy, opium, nights,
Give me your lips where love struts her pavan;
When towards you my passions depart in caravan
Your gaze is the shade where my cares find repose.

From those coal-black eyes, the chimneys of your soul,
O pitiless demon, less flames I implore;
I am not the Styx to nine times you enclose,

Alas! I can't quell your merciless desire
Nor calm your restless rage, Megaerian libertine –
And in the hell of your bed become Queen Proserpine!

(Translated by Patrick Gregory)

TRESSES

O fleece, tumbling to bare shoulders!
O locks! O perfume lingering drowsily,
Ecstasy! To fill tonight this darkened alcove
With memories sleeping in this hair,
Like a handkerchief, I'd wave it in the air.

Torrid Africa, and Asia's languid spell,
Whole worlds, absent, moribund, far away,
Within your depths, o fragrant forest, dwell;
As other souls drift on music's swell
Mine, o my love, on your perfume sways.

I'll go to lands where sap in man and tree
Mounts high in the burning heat, swoons and pales;
Strong tresses, be the wave that carries me!
A blinding vision is contained within this ebony sea:
Masts and oarsmen, flames, and sails:

A bustling harbor, where my soul drinks draughts
[untold
Of perfumes, colors, cries,
Where vessels glide through moire and gold,
Unfolding their vast arms to hold
The pure sky's glory, where shimmering heat-waves
[rise.

I'll plunge my loving head, that reels with drunkenness,
In this black ocean where the other is becalmed,
My subtle spirit, in the ocean tide's caress,
Will discover thee again, o fecund idleness,
Cradled in the boundless deep, where leisure lies
[embalmed!

49

Blue hair, shadow-curtained tent,
Closing round me once again azure skies afar,
Along its downy fringes, tangled, opulent,
I breathe, intoxicated, the mingled scent
Of oil of coco, musk, and tar.

Long! Forever! within your heavy mane
My hand will shower sapphires, pearls, rubies,
To bind you to my wishes; will you not remain
The oasis where I dream, the gourd from which I drain,
In long slow sips, the wine of memories?

(Translated by Helen R. Lane)

LE LÉTHÉ

Unfeeling, cruel soul, dear tigress, come,
rest on my heart, monster of indolent mien;
with my trembling fingers a long time
I'd plumb the thickness of your heavy mane,

and bury in your skirts my aching head,
as in a shroud scented with your perfume,
and breathe there, as from some long-faded bloom,
the moldy sweetness of my love now dead.

More than life itself, I want to sleep!
in an ambiguous death, in a long stupor,
with kisses, in which no remorse shall creep,
spent on your lovely body polished like copper.

To bury my stilled sobbing, nothing's worth
more to me than your deep bed's abyss;
a great oblivion dwells on your mouth,
and Lethe's tide flows in me with your kiss.

My fate shall be my one delight in future,
like one of the elect, I shall obey;
a martyr, damned but innocent, I'll pray
fervently to stir up fires of torture.

I'll suck, to drown the rancor of my hurt,
nepenthe and hemlock laden with rest
from the charming nipples of these pointed breasts
that have never been the wardens of a heart.

(Translated by C. F. MacIntyre)

MADAME SABATIER

The poems dedicated to Mme Sabatier are as different from those inspired by Jeanne Duval as is a cool brook from a steaming geyser. When, by rare exception, the tone of these poems catches fire, it is the poet's, not Mme Sabatier's, character that has gained the upper hand. Among the ten or twelve poems of the *Fleurs du Mal* which can be attributed to the inspiration of the gorgeous "Présidente," there is only one that can be considered to be truly passionate: "À Celle qui est trop gaie," which the smutty-minded magistrates of the criminal court immediately branded as obscene.

We know that most of these poems, as soon as they were written, were sent to Mme Sabatier, anonymously, by the poet. "À Celle qui est trop gaie" was, indeed, the very first of the series. We can imagine Mme Sabatier's surprise on finding, amidst her morning mail, those amorous verses accompanied by a brief note that the poet had scrawled out in a disguised hand:

The person for whom these verses were written, whether they please her or displease her (even if she finds them utterly ridiculous), is humbly *beseeched* not to show them to *anyone*. Deep sentiments have a strong sense of modestly. The absence of any signature, is that not invincible proof of that modesty? The person who wrote these verses, in one of those frequent fits of reverie brought on by the image of her who inspired them, loves this creature with all his heart, without ever having told her so, and will *always* have for her the tenderest regard. (Letter of December 10, 1852.)

À CELLE QUI EST TROP GAIE

Your gestures, head, and grace
with a lovely landscape vie;

51

laughter plays on your face
like a cool wind in a clear sky.

Your little troubles dance
off, dazzled by the charm
of health's clear radiance
from your shoulders and arms.

The sonorous colors that gleam,
sprangling your dresses' array,
would make any poet dream
of flowers in a ballet.

And these mad costumes prove
the motley of your brains;
mad woman for whom I'm insane,
I hate you as much as I love.

When I dragged my debility
sometimes in a garden to rest,
I have felt the irony
Of sunlight tearing my breast;

the springtime and its verdure
so humbled me with their power
that I have punished Nature's
insolence in a flower.

Also, I'd like, some night
when sounds the hour of pleasure,
to steal to your body's treasures,
like a coward with footsteps light,

to whip your flesh, so frank,
and bruise the forgiven mound
of your breast, in your startled flank
to cut a broad deep wound,

and then, with dizzy rapture,
in those lips, shining and new,
I would infuse in you
my venom, O my sister!

(Translated by C. F. MacIntyre)

MADAME SABATIER
Bust by Clesinger (Louvre).

Apollonie Sabatier, when she received this rather unusual love-letter, was thirty-one years of age, just two days short of being a full year younger than Baudelaire. Lavishly provided for by the son of a banker, she used to receive at her flat, on the Rue Frochot, at the corner of the Place de la Barrière-Montmartre (today Place Pigalle), a great number of artists and writers. All who met her were in agreement with Judith Gautier who stated that "three graces shone from her: beauty, goodness, and joy." For her, living was a pleasure.

In December, 1852 when Baudelaire, under cover of anonymity, assured Mme Sabatier of his "tenderest regard," he was among her most assiduous, if not among her most familiar, visitors. We can not say whether she immediately guessed the identity of her passionate correspondent, but it would not be rash to assume that she did not remain long in doubt.

In May, 1853 she received two poems, again unsigned, within a single week. Both these poems were later to be included in the *Fleurs du Mal* under the titles "Réversibilité" and "Confession." To this latter poem her correspondent joined a brief note in which he attempted to excuse his cowardly anonymity:

Truly, Madame, I ask your forgiveness for this idiotic anonymous doggerel which seems so horribly childish; but what am I to do? Like children and invalids, I am a dreadful egoist. When I am suffering my thoughts go out to those whom I love. My thoughts about you are usually in verse, and when these verses have been put down on paper I can not resist the temptation to send them back to their source of inspiration. At the same time, I hide away like someone who has a true terror of ridicule. Is there not something essentially comic about love? Especially for those who have not fallen a victim to it.

But I swear to you that this is the last time that I shall expose myself; and if my ardent affection for you lasts as long as it had already before I even mentioned it to you, we will both be overtaken by old age.

However absurd all this may appear to you, keep

in mind that it would be extremely cruel to make light of this heart of mine – this heart that shall always cherish your image.

His resolution to no longer "expose" himself was soon broken. In February, 1854 the flow of anonymous epistles was resumed. In less than ten days Mme Sabatier received three sonnets which were, like the preceding poems, to appear later in the *Fleurs du Mal*. We shall quote the last of the three in which the poet expresses his need for some sort of spiritual protection, a persistent theme with Baudelaire as his *My Heart Laid Bare* clearly demonstrates. In his intimate journals he vows to pray every morning "to his father, to Mariette, to Poe, as intermediaries." And here the poet turns to his idealized mistress for aid and comfort:

What will you say tonight, poor solitary Soul,
What will you find to say, my withered, hungry Heart,
to the most-Beautiful, most-Good, to the most-dearly-
[Beloved,
Whose divine apparition has restored you to life?

– We will teach our proud voice to sing her acclaim,
For nothing compares to the sweetness of her reign;
Her sacred flesh is scented with Angelic perfume
And her eye enshrouds us in robes of light.

Whether it be at night, in the depths of solitude,
Whether it be in the streets, amidst the multitude,
Her Phantom walks, dancing like a Flame.

Sometimes it speaks, saying: "I am *Beautiful*, and
[decree
That for love of *ME*, only *Beauty* shall you love.
I am the Guardian Angel, the Muse, and the Madonna.
(Translated by Patrick Gregory)

A strange interplay of coyness and modesty prevented both Baudelaire and Mme Sabatier from ever referring to these poems before the trial of the *Fleurs du Mal*, although their author had finally revealed his identity when, in 1855, he sent two of them, with his signature, to the *Revue des Deux Mondes* for publication. Still, it was only after the seizure of the *Fleurs du Mal* that Mme Sabatier received, for the first time, a letter from him in his own hand:

Would you believe that those wretches (I refer to the judge, the prosecuting attorney, etc.) have dared to incriminate, among other pieces, two of the poems that I wrote for my beloved idol? . . .

This is the first time I have written you in my own handwriting. If I were not at the moment so over-burdened with business and letters (the hearing is tomorrow) I would take advantage of this occasion to beg your forgiveness for my many childish follies. But then, haven't you been sufficiently avenged, especially by that little sister of yours? Oh, the little monster! She caught sight of me one day and turned me into ice by bursting out in laughter, right in my face, and saying: "Are you still pining after my sister and sending her such magnificent letters?" I understood then that I had been doing a very poor job of concealing my identity, and that your charming face disguises a spirit that is something less than charitable. Boors may "pine" after their loved ones but poets *idolize* them. And I do not think that your little sister is inclined to comprehend such lofty conceptions.

Now, at the risk of making you laugh as well, let me repeat those vows that caused such merriment to that little imp. Try to imagine a *pot pourri* of longing, affection, respect, mixed with a thousand nonsensical sentiments that are deadly serious, and there you have that very sincere something that I am quite unable to express any better.

To forget you is impossible. I have heard it said that there have been some poets who have never let their thoughts stray one moment from the image of the woman they loved. I indeed believe (but then, I am only too prejudiced) *that fidelity is one of the signs of true genius.*

You are more than my beloved and cherished dream, you are my *superstition.* When I commit some idiotic blunder, I say to myself: "My god! If she ever knew about that!" When I do something worthwhile, I say: "There's something that brings me a little closer to her – in spirit."

And the last time that I had the good fortune to see you (quite in spite of myself, for I flee your approach) I was saying to myself: "Now wouldn't it be strange if that carriage were waiting there for *her*; perhaps I had better turn down another street." – And then: *"Good evening, Monsieur!"* in that beloved voice that both enchants me and tears me apart. And I wandered off, repeating all the way home: "Good evening, Monsieur!," trying to recapture the exact tone of your voice.

Adieu, dear Madame, I kiss your hands with all my devotion.

The epilogue to this strange love affair is too well known to linger over, and although it undoubtedly deserves a prominent place in the poet's biography, it is of little importance in an appreciation of his poetry. It can even be said that, by stepping into the inner circle of Baudelaire's existence, on August 30, 1957, Mme Sabatier forfeited her position as the poet's Muse. On the very next day she received what is probably one of the strangest and most disquieting letters that ever flowed from the pen of a requited lover. With heartrending nonchalance he switches from terms of endearment to playful banter, from tenderness to cynicism:

I said to you yesterday: You will soon forget me, you will desert me, he who pleases you today will bore you tomorrow. And I add now: he alone will suffer who, like a fool, takes seriously the antics of the soul. You see, my very beautiful darling, I have odious prejudices as far as women are concerned. In short, I lack faith. You have a beautiful soul, but when all is said and done, it is a woman's soul.

... And lastly, lastly, a few days ago you were a divinity, which was so nice, so charming, so permanent. And now you are a woman.

... In short, let events take their course. I have

57

always been something of a fatalist. But what I know for a fact is that I have a horror of passion – because I am acquainted with all its degradations – and now I see the beloved idol that reigned supreme over my life becoming too seductive.

I don't dare reread this letter. I would probably be forced to alter it, for I have a genuine fear of afflicting you, and it seems to me that I have brought to the surface the bad side of my character.

From these few extracts, it is easy to see why such a profession, not of faith, but of an absence of faith, has given rise to so much comment. As for Mme Sabatier, she believed that she was being scorned for Jeanne Duval, and between the pages of her copy of the *Fleurs du Mal* she slipped a portrait of her rival drawn by Baudelaire's own hand, and scribbled beneath it the inscription: "His ideal!" She was mistaken, but how are we to disentangle the whole truth? There are too many explanations for this broken liaison and perhaps none of them is entirely satisfactory. Perhaps Baudelaire simply emerged from this affair as one emerges from a dream. He was certainly born a person not-quite-of-this-world, and he was always to remain that way.

THE TWO FOOLS

In *My Heart Laid Bare* Baudelaire states that his feeling of solitude, his awareness of being a creature apart from the crowd, dates from a very early age:

> Feeling of solitude since my childhood. In spite of my family – and often amidst my comrades – a feeling of being predestined for eternal solitude.

It seems certain that the loss of his father in 1827 and especially the remarriage of his mother in the following year were to have a great deal to do with the birth of this feeling that was, with time, to grow into a conviction and to affect his whole outlook on existence.

The solitude of his home – a home that had, in his opinion, ceased to be his after the intrusion of the Commander Aupick – was soon succeeded by the solitude of boarding-school where it would have been a miracle if his unstable temperament had permitted him to form any close friendships among his classmates. Condemned to loneliness, and vaguely convinced that this condemnation was beyond appeal, he behaved as though he were absolutely determined to isolate himself from the world and made a strangely methodical effort to cut himself off from all society – family, school, professional, political.

Such an attitude could not, of course, be rigorously maintained, and in both his life and writings we frequently come across a Baudelaire who has cast aside his role as a reprobate, or as that diligent egoist that he chose to call a *dandy*. But it is nonetheless true that this solitude – at first endured, and later defiantly accepted – inspired and nourished the essential part of his work.

Neither love nor art was to vanquish his loneliness. Nor were they to overcome his pride in standing alone.

On the contrary, this awareness of his isolation and of the unusual benefits that he drew from it made him regard all forms of social intercourse – whether in politics, art, or love – as a sort of personal *prostitution:* a word which in Baudelaire's vocabulary lost none of its perjorative force even though he often used it in an abstract sense, without reference to venality and the flesh.

Although he has written in *Fusées* that "love is the taste for prostitution," it does not follow – far from it – that he believed that love constitutes a total abandon or giving over of the self. On the contrary, in *My Heart Laid Bare* he denounces the dupery that accompanies the communion of two lovers:

> In love, as in almost all human affairs, the mutual agreement is the result of a misunderstanding. And the cause of this misunderstanding is Pleasure. The man cries out: "Oh my angel!" The woman coos: "Mama, Mama!" And the two fools are convinced that their thoughts are in harmony. The impassable abyss, caused by an inability to communicate. still gapes between them.

But if love is not a gift of the self, the supreme gesture of generosity, then it must be a *natural* function of man, that is to say, a thing tarnished by *sin*. It is this conviction of the fundamental sinfulness of love that pervades all Baudelaire's work, that gives voice to a deep-rooted misogamy which is all the more agonizing to the reader because one feels that the poet's appetite for the "world of women" has never released its tyrannical hold on him.

In *Fusées* we read:

> I believe that I have already remarked somewhere that love bears a strong resemblance to torture or to a surgical operation. But this idea can be further developed in all its implied bitterness. Even when two lovers are very deeply in love and full of reciprocal desires, one of them will always be calmer or less possessed than the other. And he, or she, shall be the surgeon or torturer; the other shall be the patient or

victim. Do you hear those sighs, the prelude to a tragedy of dishonor; those moans, those cries, those death-rattles? Who has not uttered them, who has not instinctively extorted them from the victim? And would you find anything worse in the most skillful "interrogation" of a master torturer? Those eyes of a convulsed somnambulist, those limbs that quiver and writhe as though under the pressure of a pile-driver – opium, drunkenness, delirium, in their most furious stages can not produce such frightening, such fascinating results. And the human face, which Ovid believed was fashioned to reflect the stars, now expresses naught but insane ferocity, or collapses into an image of death. For I would most certainly consider it a sacrilege to apply the word "ecstasy" to this sort of decomposition.

Terrifying game where one of the players is obliged to lose all control over himself!

One day, among friends, someone brought up the question of what constituted the greatest pleasure of love. One person replied with great frankness: to receive; and another: to give one's self. This one said: the pleasure of pride!; that one said: the voluptuousness of humility! The whole stinking lot babbled like the *Imitation of Christ*. Finally an impudent utopian affirmed that the greatest pleasure of love was to manufacture new citizens for the State.

As for me, I declare that the only and supreme joy of love comes from the certitude of doing *evil*. And all men and women know from birth that all sensual delights stem from evil.

And in *My Heart Laid Bare*:

There exists in every man, at every moment of his life, two impulses simultaneously at work: one toward God, the other toward Satan. The invocation to God, or spirituality, asserts a desire to ascend; the invocation to Satan, or bestiality, is the joy of descending. It is to the latter that we must attribute man's love for women, and for all intimate conversations with beasts, dogs, cats, etc.

A MUSEUM OF LOVE

It should be kept in mind that the texts we have just cited belong to the last ten years of Baudelaire's life, the darkest period of his existence: Jacques Crépet attributes *Fusées* to the years between 1855 and 1862, and *My Heart Laid Bare* to those between 1859 and 1862. But in March, 1846, that is to say, at a time when Baudelaire could write to his mother that he had never been "so full of bright hopes," he was already exhibiting that bitter disillusionment that was to engulf his later work. In a chapter of his *Salon of 1846* devoted to paintings that treat the subject of love, we come across several pages that, in spite of their humor and vivacity, can not entirely conceal the strange bitter-sweet flavor of fruit that has ripened too soon:

Has it ever been your experience, as it has been mine, to find yourself overcome by the blackest sort of melancholy after having leafed through a collection of erotic prints? Have you ever wondered from whence comes the strange fascination of the annals of the bed-chamber, hidden away at the back of bookstores, or buried under old crates and cartons? And wondered too, from whence comes the depression that they never fail to inspire? Pleasure and sadness mixed, a potion that never slakes our insatiable thirst! The pleasure comes from seeing depicted in all its forms nature's most compelling emotion – and anger from seeing this emotion so badly imitated or foolishly misunderstood. Whether it be during one of those interminable winter evenings, huddled over the fire, or during the idle hours of summer's dog-days, lost in the corner of some framing-shop, the sight of these drawings never fails to plunge me into a deep abyss of contemplation, just as an obscene book always hurls us into the mystic ocean of depression. While gazing at these countless scraps of emotion, samples of Everyman's desires, I have often found myself wishing for some sort of

63

Museum of Love where poets, philosophers, and all interested parties could wander at will, and where everything would have its place, from the almost obsolete devotion of a Saint Theresa to the pedantic excesses of the Eras of Boredom. There is most certainly an immense distance separating Watteau's *Departure for Cythera* from those wretched colored prints that hang over a cracked pitcher and a wobbly chest of drawers in a whore's bedroom; but in a study as complex and as varied as love, nothing should be neglected. And then, genius, can sanctify anything, and if these subjects were treated with the necessary care and reflection they would not be soiled by that revolting obscenity which is not veracity, but rather mere barroom swaggering.

Oh, the moralist need not take alarm; I shall know how to maintain a reasonable decorum, and, as curator, would readily content myself with the acquisition of one immense Hymn of Love drawn by only the purest hands, by Ingres, by Watteau, by Rubens, by Delacroix! The frivolous and elegant princesses of Watteau beside the serious and languid Venuses of M. Ingres; the splendid white tints of Rubens and Jordaens, and the somber beauties of Delacroix, women that invade our dreams: tall, pale women, drowned in satin.

And to further appease the ferocious chastity of my reader, I hereby affirm that my gallery will not be limited only to pictures with amorous subject-matter, but will also include every painting that breathes love, be it only a portrait.

In this immense exhibition, I envisage the beauty and love of every clime, expressed by the foremost artists; from the madcap, vaporous creatures of Watteau *fils'* fashion engravings to those Venuses of Rembrandt who trim their nails like ordinary mortals or dress their hair with a bulky wooden brush.

Pictures of this nature are so very compelling that there is no artist, great or small, who has not applied himself to them, openly or in secret, from Jules Romain to Déveria and Gavarni.

Their primary fault is, in general, that they lack

naïvety or sincerity. I recall, however, a lithograph that expresses – without too much delicacy, I'm sorry to say – one of the great truths of promiscuous love. A young man in woman's attire and his mistress, dressed as a man, are seated together on a sofa (a sofa that you could not fail to recognize, the standard model to be found in furnished flats or one-night hotels). And the young woman is coyly lifting her lover's skirt. This sumptuous passage in my imaginary museum would be balanced by many other pages where love appears only in its most delicate forms.

If we were called upon to classify this dream-museum of Baudelaire's under one of the conventional headings, there would certainly be some hesitation between putting it under ethics or aesthetics. As a matter of fact, it springs from a science that is essentially Baudelarian in its conception: Dandyism. And it is the dandy – or rather, Baudelaire's own particular idea of the dandy – that expresses himself in the above passages. Only a person of leisure and refinement (Baudelaire's alter ego Samuel Cramer, for instance) could indulge his imagination with such erudite and delicate eroticism, could conceive of this museum where the amorous adventures of Aretino, illustrated by Jules Romain and Carraccio, could be found alongside Fragonard's little flirts, Ingres' odalisques, and the caricatures of Gavarni.

Es que cette beauté, sombre comme le fer,
Est-il celles que forge et que polit l'Enfer
Par accomplir un jour de luxures
Et contrister le cœur d'humbles créatures

affaissant sous son poids, un énorme oreiller,
Un beau corps incliné, doux à voir sommeiller,
En son sommeil orné d'un sourire superbe

. . . . .

L'ornière de son dos par le défi haut.

L'air était imprégné d'une amoureuse rage;
Les insectes volaient à la lampe et nul vent
Ne faisait tressaillir le rideau ni l'auvent.
C'était une nuit chaude, un vrai bain de jouvence.

Ici, la bouche est meilleure.
D'ailleurs, même observation.

BAUDELAIRE: SELF-PORTRAIT
*Poulet-Malassis wrote of this sketch: "This is the best likeness of him that I
know of. It dates from 1860. Compare this drawing—and the author's commentary—with the drawing reproduced on p. 4.*

THE DANDY

But what exactly was Baudelaire's conception of the dandy? The word frequently flows from his pen, and we know that he one day intended to write a long essay on its meaning. Although this essay was never to be written, Baudelaire has at least left us several pages in his study of the painter Constantin Guys, *The Painter of Contemporary Life,* in which he speaks at length on the subject of dandyism.

These pages deserve our attention and have a definite significance in any study of the poet, for although the dandy, as Baudelaire describes him, has at his disposal an abundance of both money and leisure (which was certainly not the case with Baudelaire), it is perfectly clear that this rare and intriguing creature is a projection of an ideal Baudelaire, conceived by himself.

The dandy, or Baudelaire the Millionaire:

The man who, wealthy, independent, even a bit blasé, has no other occupation than to pursue happiness; the man brought up amid luxury and accustomed from birth to the obedience of other men, in short, the man whose sole profession is personal elegance, will always posses, in all ages of history, a distinctive physiognomy, will always be readily distinguishable from the herd. Dandyism is a vague sort of institution, as peculiar as dueling; very ancient, since Caesar, Catilina, Alcibiades furnish us with striking prototypes; very widespread, since Chateaubriand found it flourishing amidst the forests and along the lakes of the New World. Dandyism, which is an institution beyond the law, nonetheless has laws of its own to which the dandy must rigorously adhere, no matter how capricious, no matter how independent his character. The

English novelists have, above all others, cultivated the novel of "high-life," and the French writers who, like M. de Custine, have devoted their efforts to producing modern romances, have first of all – and quite judiciously – taken pains to endow their heroes with large enough fortunes to pay for their most extravagant flights of fancy, and have seen to it that they are not tied down by any sort of profession. These creatures have no other duty in life than to cultivate, in their person, an ideal of beauty, than to satisfy their passions, than to feel and think. They possess, according to their needs and desires, vast amounts of both time and money, without which fancy, reduced to a state of fleeting day-dreams, can never be transformed into action. It is unfortunately all too true that without leisure and money love can be nothing more than a rather sordid orgy, or the dutiful accomplishment of a domestic chore. Instead of being a flaming impulse, or delicately conceived caprice, it becomes a repugnant *utility*.

If I speak of love in connection with dandyism, it is because love is the natural occupation of men of leisure. But the dandy does not regard love as his sole goal. If I speak of money, it is because money is an indispensable prerequisite for those who wish to make a cult of their passions. But the dandy does not aspire after money as a thing in itself: indefinite credit is good enough for him, and he abandons that filthy passion for lucre to vulgar mortals. Dandyism is not, as many shallow-minded people seem to think, merely an immoderate taste for fine dress and elegant surroundings. Those things are for the true dandy only the symbols of the aristocratic superiority of his spirit. And what is more, to his eyes, always eagerly seeking for true *distinction*, perfection in attire consists of absolute simplicity, which is, undoubtedly, the best way to distinguish oneself. What then is this passion which, become a doctrine, has acquired such notable converts, this charterless institution which has formed such a lofty caste of men? Above all, it is a burning need for individuality, contained within the outermost boundaries of social convention. It is a sort of cult of the self, the self that can survive that search for happiness that we seek in others, in women for example; which can even survive that which we call illusions. It is the pleasure of provoking astonishment, and the proud satisfaction of never being astonished. A dandy may be a blasé man, he may be a man who has undergone a great deal of suffering, but in the latter case, he will always suffer in silence, like the Spartan youth who concealed a fox under his cloak.

One can see that dandyism, through certain sides of its nature, verges on a stoical and spiritual doctrine. Above all, a dandy can never be vulgar. If he commits a crime, that does not necessarily mean a fall from grace, but if that crime springs from a trivial motive, the resulting dishonor is without appeal. Let the reader not be too scandalized by this grave concern over frivolous things, and let him remember that there is a certain grandeur in all follies, a certain strength in all excesses. Strange spiritualism! For those who are both its priests and victims, all the complex material conditions which they must submit to, from the impeccable attire both day and night, to the perilous risks of the game, are only a sort of gymnastic exercise designed to fortify the will and discipline the soul. In fact, I was not entirely wrong to consider dandyism as a sort of religion. The rules of the most rigorous monastic order, the irrevocable commands of the Old Man of the Mountain who compelled his drunken disciples to commit suicide, were not more despotic, were not more obediently adhered to than this doctrine of elegance and individuality which imposes on its ambitious and humble aspirants, men often full of fire, passion, and courage, men charged with repressed energy, the terrible formula: *Perinde ac cadaver*!

Whether these men call themselves aesthetes, sceptics, beaux, lions, or dandies, all of them issue from the same source, all share the same character of revolt and opposition, all represent the best aspect of human pride – that need (all too rare today) to wage war against, and destroy, triviality. From this compulsion springs the dandy's awareness of caste and his haughty bearing, provoking even in its frigidity. Dandyism flourishes especially in periods of transition, when democracy is not yet all-powerful and the aristocracy is just beginning to totter and decay. Amidst the turmoil of these times, a small group of men, *déclassés*, at loose-ends, fed-up – but all of them rich in determination – will conceive the idea of founding a new sort of aristocracy, stronger than the old, for it shall be based on only the most precious, the most indestructible factors, on those Heaven-sent gifts that neither money nor ambition can confer. Dandyism represents the last burst of heroism of a decadent society; and the sort of dandy found by the voyager in North America in no way invalidates this idea, for there is no reason to suppose that those tribes of what we choose to call "savages" are not the tattered remnants of some great civilization. Dandyism is a setting sun; like the great star that sinks below the horizon, it is superb, but without warmth and full of melancholy. But alas! the rising tide of democracy that engulfs all, that levels everything, is day by day drowning these last representatives of human pride, and pouring its floods of oblivion over these prodigious Myrmidons. Here in France dandies are becoming ever more rare, while across the water in England the social structure and constitution of that country (a real constitution, a constitution based on the tradition and manners of the people) will for many years to come provide a home for the successors of Sheridan, Brummell and Byron, if any legitimate heirs ever happen to appear on the scene.

The essay on Guys from which these pages are taken was written at the end of 1859 and during the first weeks of 1860. Evidence of Baudelaire's preoccupation with dandyism can also be found in *Fusées* and *My Heart Laid Bare,* both works contemporary or posterior to the essay. Thus it can be said that the subject continued to fascinate the poet up until the very last years of his life. Moreover, his customary behavior in public reveals that no matter how urgent, how maddening, his need for money may have been, there was nothing that caused him more torment than this constant effort to maintain, even under the most trying circumstances, that air of distinction that makes the dandy a true prince of the spirit.

In *My Heart Laid Bare* he has written:

> DANDYISM. – What is a superior man? Not the specialist. It is the man of leisure and of broad background.

And a little farther on:

> It is by leisure that I have, in part, gained stature.
> To my great detriment; for leisure, without an income, breeds debts, and the snubs that result from debts.
> But to my great advantage, in terms of sensitivity, of meditation, and of the resources of dandyism and dilettantism.

His great variety of interests and his irrepressible inclination for idleness, would they thus have made him into the dandy that he longed to be if Fortune had seen fit to furnish him with an income? Not entirely, for that all-important attribute of the true dandy, absolute impassivity, was lacking from his nature. When he wrote in *My Heart Laid Bare:* "The dandy must aspire to be perpetually sublime; he must live and sleep in front of a mirror," Baudelaire was not describing himself as he was, but as he would have liked to have been.

BASH HIM DOWN, THE ENEMY OF ROSES!

The antonym of dandy, the exact opposite of that singular and cultivated creature, is the mob, the masses, the people (the bourgeoisie being quite obviously included in this category). And thus it is not entirely surprising that Baudelaire's voice should bristle with disdain when he turns his attention to the multitude:

> Can you imagine a dandy addressing the people for any other reason than to express his scorn for them? *(My Heart Laid Bare)*
> ... And the people, who adore the degradation of the whip. *(Fleurs du Mal,* "Le voyage")
> The true saint is he who whips and slaughters the people for the good of the people. *(Fusées)*

As his notebooks clearly reveal, Baudelaire was deeply impressed by the writings of Joseph de Maistre, whose biting style, impertinent tone, and misogyny seemed to have been specially tailored to suit the poet's own taste. In his introduction to Poe's *Nouvelles Histoires extraordinaires* Baudelaire quotes, with obvious delight, a remark of the American writer: "The people have nothing to do with the laws except to obey them. The nose of the populace is its imagination; for one need only grab hold of it by this nose in order to lead it about with ease." Elsewhere, in his *Fusées,* he has jotted down: "De Maistre and Edgar Poe have taught me how to reason."

His horror of democracy is so profound, that he uses some of the strangest sort of arguments to nourish his prejudice. For example, in *Fusées* we come across the passage:

> It is easy to guess why democrats do not like cats. Cats are beautiful; they give one an idea of luxury, of cleanliness, of voluptuousness, etc.

There is a certain temptation to attribute this attitude of Baudelaire's to the repeated rebuffs he received from the public, to the condemnation of his *Fleurs du Mal,*

73

and, above all, to the general lack of comprehension that greeted the publication of any and all of his works. It is perfectly understandable that these continual setbacks should have served to reinforce his convictions, but they did nothing more than reinforce them. Even in the days when "hope still shimmered at the windows of the inn," that is to say, during the spring of 1846 when he was spending his inheritance in a sort of ecstatic delirium, he was submitting for publication certain pages that in no way contradict the ferocious aphorisms of his later years.

Eighteen forty-six was also the year of his *Salon,* and the general vulgarity of the pictures at the exhibition provoked him into expressing his deep scorn for the masses, the enemy of Beauty; scorn which, it is true, is expressed with more irony, more buffoonery, than genuine bitterness – but scorn, nonetheless:

Have you ever experienced (those of you whose inclination for idle strolling has sometimes led you into the midst of a street-brawl) the same delight as I have felt in watching a Guardian of the Public Sleep – a member of the town or municipal police, the true soldiers of the State – beat up a Republican? And like me, have you ever cried out in your heart of hearts: "Bash him down, hit him a little harder! bash him! bash him! sweet policeman of my heart's desire, for when you bring down your magnificent club, I adore you and consider you the equal of great Jupiter, the Lawgiver. That man whom you are bashing is an enemy of Watteau, an enemy of Raphaël, a bitter enemy of luxury, of the beaux-arts and belles lettres, a sworn iconoclast, the beheader of Venus and Apollo! He no longer wants to be the humble and anonymous workman cultivating roses and perfuming the public; he wants to be free, the ignorant wretch, and he is utterly incapable of founding a greenhouse or fabricating a new scent. Lay it on with devotion! Belabor the anarchists' shoulders!

Likewise all true philosophers and critics should bring down their compassionless clubs on these apes of art, these emancipated laborers who hate the strength and sovereignty of genius. *(Salon of 1846)*

THE ATTRACTION OF DUPONT

By a curious coincidence, the year 1846, which witnessed the publication of Baudelaire's polemic against the "Republicans," was also the year in which we find him deeply moved by the misery of the working classes. Has he actually rallied to the banner of Fraternity, even before Hugo adopted the cause? In any case, his article on his friend, the café singer Pierre Dupont, presents us with a very disconcerting sort of Baudelaire: unfaithful to himself, to his aesthetic, to his poetry, to his taste for solitude and solitary musings – unfaithful to everything, one could say, save to his friendship for Dupont!

It is no longer a question of beating down the "humble and anonymous laborer" but, on the contrary, of presenting him with those very roses that the lout now refuses to cultivate for the adornment of the dandy's *boutonnière*. Let us listen for a moment to Baudelaire the socialist as he recounts his conversion which took place during a recital of Dupont's verses:

> When I first heard this magnificent cry of anguish and melancholy (*Le Chant des Ouvriers*, 1846) I was astounded and deeply moved. For a good many years now we have been waiting for a bit of poetry that has both vitality and truth! It is impossible – no matter what social group one may belong to, no matter what prejudices one may have been nourished on – to remain untouched by the vision of this sickly multitude breathing in the dust of the workshop, choking on lint, impregnated with lead, mercury, and the other poisons that are necessary for the creation of masterpieces, sleeping amid vermin, in the lowliest quarters of the city where the humblest and most magnificent virtues abide side by side with the vilest vices and the refuse

from the galleys; by the vision of this sighing, languishing multitude to whom "the world owes its splendor," which feels "a bright red blood surge through its veins," which casts a longing glance, full of sorrow, on the sun and shadows of the great parks, and which, for its sole aid and consolation, cries out its never-ceasing refrain of redemption: *Let us love one another!*

Dupont looked about him and discovered his destiny; he had only to walk straight ahead down the path before him. To tell of the joys, the pains, and the dangers of the worker's lot, and to shed a little light on all the various aspects, all the diverse horizons of human suffering and toil, with the aid of a comforting philosophy, such was the task he took upon himself and faithfully accomplished. The time will come when this Marseillaise of Labor will fly from lip to lip like some Masonic pass-word, and when the exile, the refugee, the lost voyager, be he under the devouring sky of the tropics or amidst deserts of snow, will sense the air perfumed by this invigorating refrain:

> We whose lamp in the morning
> At the cock's first cry takes flame,
> Who must part before the dawning
> For wretched wages and shame,

and will say to himself: I have nothing more to fear; I am in France.

. . . What is the great secret of Dupont's success, whence comes the irresistible attraction of his work? This great (yet very simple) secret, let me reveal it to you: it is in neither his training, nor his ingenuity; in neither his craftsmanship, nor in the various and sundry processes by which an artist taps the sources of human knowledge; no, it is in Dupont's profound love of virtue and humanity, and in an indefinable something which emanates from his poetry that I would choose to call a boundless predilection for the Republic.

It is somewhat startling to compare these lines on Dupont's altruism, on the irresistible attraction of his

BAUDELAIRE, BY MANET

overflowing heart, with Baudelaire's sarcastic commentary on an inscription that Hugo had written for him in a presentation copy of the Great Man's *Chanson des rues et des bois*: "To Charles Baudelaire, *jungamus dextras*":

> That, I believe, does not simply mean: "Let's shake hands." I know how to read between the lines of Hugo's Latin. What he is driving at is: "Let's join hands to save the human race." But I don't give a damn about the human race and he can't see that. (Letter to Edouard Manet, October 28, 1865).

But neither in 1846 when he first fell under the spell of Dupont's *Chant des Ouvriers,* nor in 1851 when he wrote his enthusiastic article on the balladier had he yet learned from de Maistre "how to reason." He yielded as he always did, even in his most contemplative moments, to the need to interpret his emotions and he succumbed entirely to the charms – he still recalled the experience in 1861 – of Dupont himself singing his plaintive melodies.

77

DRAWINGS BY BAUDELAIRE
Right: *Champfleury, who in Febru-*
ary, 1848, was the "editor-owner"
—along with Baudelaire and Toubin
—of Le Salut Public (The Public
Welfare), *a daily. (Two numbers*
were published.)
Below: *Two profiles of Blanqui, who*
drafted a constitution which for a
time (February, 1848) aroused Bau-
delaire's enthusiasm. (The hand-
written notation is by Poulet-
Malassis.)

BE ALWAYS DRUNK

The events of February, 1848 acted on Baudelaire in an analogous manner: he was seduced by the revolution just as he had been seduced by a song. On the evening of the 24th one of his friends caught sight of the poet at the Carrefour de Buci amidst a group of rioters that had just finished looting a gunsmith's shop. He was brandishing, says Jules Buisson, "a handsome double-barrelled rifle, and wore a superb yellow leather cartridge case slung over his shoulder." Thus equipped, he proclaimed loudly that he was off "to shoot down General Aupick!" A behavior scarcely in keeping with his role as a phlegmatic dandy.

Although it is undoubtedly true that many of his friends were to be found in the Republican camp at this time, it does not seem that they can be held in any way responsible for influencing his conduct during those mad days of '48. No, it seems that he had simply abandoned himself to one of those feverish fits of intoxication that he speaks of in one of his *Petits Poèmes en prose,* "Enivrez-vous" ("Get drunk"):

> You must be always drunk. That is the whole secret, that is the – one and only – question. In order not to feel the horrible burden of Time that breaks your shoulders and bends you to the ground, you must be continually drunk.
>
> But drunk on what? On wine, on poetry, on virtue – whatever you wish. But get drunk.

In February, 1848 Baudelaire "got drunk" on Republicanism. And his intoxication was doubtless increased by the thought that he might find the opportunity to take a pot-shot at his stepfather General Aupick, who had, thanks to the patronage of the Orléans princes, recently received a series of rapid promotions and was now Superintendent of the École Polytechnique.

As he later confessed in his *My Heart Laid Bare,* his behavior during February, 1848 was not motivated by any political convictions:

[handwritten manuscript facsimile]

My state of intoxication in 1848.
What was the nature of this intoxication?
Taste for vengeance. *Natural* pleasure of destruction.
Literary intoxication; memory of readings.

He even went so far as to look upon this revolution as an event that was "charming in its excess of ridiculousness."

We know nothing of his attitude concerning the *coup d'état* of December, 1851 except for the three lines in *My Heart Laid Bare:*

[handwritten manuscript facsimile]

My fury at the *coup d'état.* How many musket shots I brushed off. Another Bonaparte!
What shame!

ONLY THIEVES ARE CONVINCED

From what we can glean here and there from his writings, it seems that Baudelaire's interest in politics was only intermittent and that he generally managed to remain wholly detached from happenings around him, regarding them with the scornful aloofness of a bystander. In a letter of March 5, 1852 he wrote to the supervisor of his estate, Monsieur Ancelle, who was at that time mayor of Neuilly and a candidate for re-election:

> You did not see me at the polls; my absence was deliberate. December 2nd stripped me of all political sentiments. General ideas no longer exist. That all Paris is Orleanist is a fact, but that has nothing to do with me. If I had voted, I could have voted only for myself. Perhaps the future belongs to men outside the social hierarchy?

Henceforth, he will never be seen to wave in his conviction that one should studiously avoid all groups, all factions, be they political, philosophical, or literary. In February, 1848 he had supported Blanqui's scheme for a "Republican Central Committee," but he withdrew his allegiance several days later when the Committee became a reality. After the 2nd of December he took care never to involve himself in any such foolhardy projects. The very idea that anyone should want to belong to a group, any sort of group whatsoever, exasperated him. At the end of 1855, infuriated, as one can well believe, by a manifesto written by Champfleury in which his name was linked with the novelist's and Courbet's as one of the partisans of the Realist school, Baudelaire sat down and drew up the outline for an article to be called "Since Realism is . . ." in which he clearly expressed his disdain for all "schools" and his determination not to be conscripted into anybody's brigade:

> Every creator of a faction finds himself, by the very nature of things, in bad company.
>
> The most laughable errors and misunderstandings have taken place. It has been said that I myself have had the honor ... although I have always done my very best not to merit such honors.
>
> Besides, I would be – I hereby give warning to all factions – a sad sort of asset. I have a total lack of conviction, obedience, and stupidity.

It is evidently this total lack of conviction that prompted him to write in *My Heart Laid Bare:*

> I understand why one deserts a cause in order to find out what it feels like to serve another.

He intended to comment on and justify this trait of his character, and farther on in the same work we come across the rough outline of this undelivered defense:

> POLITICS. – I have no convictions, as men of this country understand the word, because I have no ambitions.
>
> I can find in myself no basis for a conviction.
>
> There is a certain cowardice, or rather, a certain softness in men of good intentions.
>
> Only thieves are convinced – of what? – that they must succeed. And so – they succeed.
>
> Why should I succeed since I haven't any desire to try?
>
> Glorious empires can be founded on crime and noble religions on imposture.
>
> However, I do possess several convictions, in the highest sense of the word, which can not be understood by men of my time.

BAUDELAIRE AS PROPHET

As allusive as its meaning may be, this last sentence seems to indicate that Baudelaire's "several convictions" are not of a political, but rather of a moral nature. Perhaps nothing affords us a clearer vision into his innermost thoughts than the most lengthy and important of the fragments gathered together in the posthumous volume entitled *Fusées*:

> The world is coming to an end. The only reason why it could continue to endure is that it exists. And what a feeble reason that is when compared with all the others that proclaim the contrary, particularly this one: what future role has the world to play under the panoply of the heavens? For supposing that the world should continue to exist, materially, would that be an existence worthy of the word and of the log-book of history? I do not say that the world will be reduced to the expedients, to the clownish chaos of the South American republics, that we will perhaps revert to a state of stark savagery and wander among the weed-covered ruins of our civilization, gun in hand, in search of pasture. No. For that fate, and its accompanying adventures, would presume that a spark of vital energy still existed, an echo of past ages. A new example and new victims of inexorable moral laws, we will perish where we thought to find life. Mechanization will have so thoroughly Americanized us, progress will have so adroitly amputated all our spiritual life, that nothing amid all the sanguinary, sacrilegious, anti-natural reveries of the utopianists will be able to compare to the final results. I challenge every thinking man to point out to me what remains of life on this earth. As for religion, I think it is utterly

useless to talk about that, to rummage among the ruins for its remains, since to take the trouble to deny the existence of God is the only way to arouse a flicker of scandal in these matters. Property has been virtually abolished with the suppression of the law of primo-geniture; but the time will come when humanity, like a vengeful ogre, will tear the last remnants from the hands of those who believed themselves to be the right-ful heirs of the revolutions. Yet that will not be the supreme misfortune.

The human imagination can, without too much diffi-culty, conceive of republics or other communal states worthy of some sort of glory if they are watched over by consecrated leaders, certain types of aristocrats. But it is not by political institutions alone that universal ruin, or universal progress – the name is of little importance – will manifest itself. It will be by the degradation of all human sentiments. Need I say that the little that remains of politics will struggle helplessly in the grip of universal bestiality, and that governments will be obliged, in order to create or to maintain a phantom of order, to resort to means which would make present-day society shudder with horror? Then the son will flee the family, not at eighteen but at twelve, emancipated by his precocious gluttony; he will flee it, not to seek heroic adventures, not to free a fair damsel from her tower captivity, not to immortalize a garret with sublime thoughts, but to found a business, to get rich, and to enter into competition with his infamous papa – founder and chief stockholder of a newspaper that spreads its light abroad and speaks of the Age as a hive of superstition. Then the women of the streets, the outcasts, those who have sampled several lovers, those who are sometimes referred to as Angels because of, out of gratitude for, the thoughtlessness that shimmers (the flame of Chance) in their existence which is as logical as evil – then these women, I say, will be looked upon as the incarnation of implacable wisdom, wisdom that will condemn everything except money, everything, even the "errors of the senses"! Then anything that resembles virtue – what am I saying! – anything that could not be considered ardent homage to Pluto, will be deemed utter folly. Justice (if in that golden era any form of justice can still be said to exist) will prosecute all citizens who have not managed to accumulate a fortune. Your wife, oh Bourgeois!, your chaste spouse whose legitimacy is the poetry of your life, will wield her legal status in the most infamously irreproachable fashion, and by appointing herself the lawful, vigilant, and devoted guardian of your cash-box, will no longer constitute your perfect ideal of the kept woman. Your daughter, with precocious nubility, will dream in her cradle that she has sold herself for a million. And as for yourself, oh Bourgeois – even less of a poet than you are today – you will find nothing to complain of, will find nothing lacking. For there are things in man that prosper and grow strong as other things wither and waste away, and thanks to the victory of progress, nothing will remain of your insides save a few knots of muscle! The times of which I speak are perhaps very near at hand; who knows whether or not they are not already with us and whether it is only the thickness of our nature that prevents us from appreciating the surroundings in which we breathe!

As for myself who sometimes sense within me the ridiculous symptoms of prophecy, I know that I shall never find a doctor to cure me. Cast astray in this villainous world, knocked about by the crowd, I resemble a man who is utterly weary, who looking back into deep recesses of the past sees nothing except disillusion and bitterness, and who looking forward into the future sees nothing save the gathering storm that brings with it nothing new in the way of misery or enlightenment. In the evening, when this man has stolen from destiny several hours of quiet pleasure, rocked in the cradle of his digestion, forgetful – as much as possible – of the past, content with the present and resigned to the future, intoxicated with his own aloofness and dandyism, proud of being not quite as base as those who pass by his window, he contemplates the smoke from his cigar and says to himself: What do I care about the fate of other men's consciences?

I am afraid that I have drifted into what men of my

profession call an *hors-d'oeuvre*. Nonetheless, I will leave these pages as they are – because I want to save some record of my present sadness.

In place of the word "sadness" that concludes this apocalyptic passage, Baudelaire had originally written the word "anger." Ernest Raynaud read into this correction a change of heart, an expression of remorse on the poet's part. Perhaps it would be wiser to attribute it to the growing weariness that overtook Baudelaire during his last years and that revealed itself in all his actions, even in all his fancies. As paralysis and death drew near, he sank ever deeper into lassitude. In the passage quoted above we see his anger giving way to sadness, just as this sadness was to give way to resignation in his daily journey toward death. Anger springs from a refusal to accept the inevitable. Perhaps this anger, which certainly dictated several of the above lines, had to be effaced before the prophecy could assume its full significance.

BEAUTY IS ALWAYS BIZARRE

Although the words Art and Beauty recur frequently in his writings, it can not be said that Baudelaire was an aesthetician in the strict sense of the word. The very titles that he chose for the collections of his critical studies – *Curiosités esthétiques* and *Bric-à-brac esthétique* – seem to indicate that he considered these works nothing more than a rough sketch of a possible aesthetic theory. Yet although he has bequeathed us no finished treatise on the subject, his writings on art reveal such a high degree of insight – and foresight – that posterity has seen fit to ratify almost all his opinions and decisions. And indeed, he is the first French writer to have spoken about painting with consistently happy results.

From his early childhood, Baudelaire's life was marked by an imperious desire for the Beautiful; one can almost say that he was domesticated by the desire for Beauty. The little boy that he evokes in his *Morale du joujou* already displays the traits of an impassioned *amateur d'art*. All children are, to a certain extent, hungry for novelty, until adolescence leads them to discover less naïve pleasure, to develop other appetites, and yet, however lively Baudelaire's taste for life and pleasure may have been at twenty, he still remained the little boy in love with brightly colored prints that we find described in the opening verses of *Voyage* – and he signed his name to numerous usury slips in order to satisfy his need for paintings and engravings. Painting was a part of his life, like poetry and love, and that is why – in contrast to so many critics who, even when they exert their utmost intellectual capacity, never relinquish the essential part of themselves – he never failed to be subjective in everything he said about art.

"Irregularity," he wrote in *Fusées*, "that is to say, the unexpected, the surprising, the shocking, is an essential part and the characteristic trait of beauty. It is hardly necessary to emphasize the importance that this idea was to assume after 1870 with the poetry of Mallarmé, Rimbaud, Corbière, and the painting of the Impressionists; but under the Second Empire, and in spite of the Romantic rebellion, in spite of Pétrus Borel and the *Bousingots,* such a statement could still be considered a startling innovation. Baudelaire elaborates and develops this theme in an essay devoted to the International Exhibition of 1855:

> It is perfectly clear to everyone that if all the men whose task it is to give expression to beauty conformed to the rules laid down by self-professed professors, beauty itself would disappear from the face of the Earth, since all the ideas, all the sensations relative to Beauty, and all their various manifestations, would be melted down into one monotonous and impersonal mass, as immense as boredom and oblivion. Variety, the *sine qua non* of life, would be effaced, so indisputably true is it that all real art, in its innumerable variations, always contains a new something that will eternally elude the regimentation and analysis of the classroom! Astonishment, which is one of the principal delights of art and literature, is dependent on this very variety of forms and sensations. The self-professed professor, a breed of mandarin-tyrant, always impresses me as being a heretic who sets himself up as God.
>
> I will go even farther, and – at the risk of offending those pompous sophists who look to books for all their wisdom – will not despair at the difficult and very delicate task of making my theory entirely clear. *Beauty is always bizarre.* I do not mean to say that it is deliberately, coldly bizarre, for in that case it would be a monster that has escaped from the confines of existence. I mean that it always contains a certain amount of strangeness, naïve strangeness, unforced and even unconscious, and that it is this strangeness that stamps it as Beautiful. It is its charter, its primary

characteristic. Reverse the proposition and try to conceive of a *banal* sort of beauty! Now, how could this strangeness, irrepressible, imcompressible, infinite in its variations, dependent on locales, on climates, on customs, on the race, religion and temperament of the artist, how could it ever be governed, restricted, put in place by the utopian regulations drawn up in a little shrine of science somewhere on this planet without art itself being put in mortal danger? This dose of strangeness, which constitutes and defines individuality, without which there can be no beauty, plays in art (and I hope that the exactitude of this comparison excuses its frivolousness) the role of taste or seasoning in cooking each dish differing from another (if we make an abstraction of their nutritive value) by the *idea* that they reveal to the tongue.

In his essay on the Salon of 1859, Baudelaire, reaffirming the principles that he had put forth four years earlier, takes care to warn his readers against certain unwarranted conclusions that had already been drawn from his ideas:

> A little while back I spoke of artists who took pains to astonish the public. The desire to astonish and to be astonished is a very legitimate one. "It is a happiness to wonder"; but too, *it is a happiness to dream.* The heart of the matter, if you expect me to confer upon you the title of artist or connoisseur of art, is to know by what process you are creating, or experiencing this astonishment. Because Beauty is *always* astonishing, it would be absurd to conclude that anything that provokes astonishment is *always* beautiful. But our noble public, which is singularly incapable of enjoying the pleasures of reverie or meditation (an indication of the triviality of its soul), wants to be astonished by means that are utterly foreign to art, and its servile artists conform to the public's taste; they attempt to attract its attention, surprise it, stupefy it by employing all sorts of lowly tricks, for they know that the public is unable to appreciate the natural interplay of true art.

As for Baudelaire's personal definition of Beauty, he has noted it down in *Fusées*. The two most learned and indefatigable Baudelaire scholars, the late Jacques Crépet and M. Georges Blin, have indeed remarked that this definition can not be considered wholly original and that Poe's influence can be readily perceived. But Baudelaire always prided himself on his affinities to Poe, and his own particular predilection for melancholy – which he borrowed from no one – is sufficient to establish the fact that the following passage is not merely an echo of his readings:

I have found the definition of Beauty, of my conception of Beauty. It is something ardent and sad, something a bit vague, leaving space for conjecture. I am now, with your permission, going to apply this idea of mine to a highly sensitive object, to what is indeed the most fascinating object in society, a woman's face. A seductive and beautiful head, that is to say, a woman's head, is a thing that makes one dream of both – but both blended in a confused sort of way – voluptuousness and sadness; which provokes as well a sentiment of melancholy, of lassitude, and yes, of satiety; or perhaps the very opposite, that is to say, a sentiment of ardor, a desire to live, associated with a recurrent tide of bitterness that seems to flow forth from sense of privation or despair. Mystery, regret, are also characteristics of Beauty.

A handsome masculine head has no need to convey, as far as other men are concerned (though women doubtless share a different viewpoint on this matter), that idea of voluptuousness which we find so very attractive in a woman's face – all the more provoking because a woman's face generally contains more melancholy than a man's. But this head will also have a certain something that is both ardent and sad: an indication of great spiritual longings, of ambitions that have been forced back into the shadows; an idea of power, held in bonds and deprived of employment; sometimes an idea of vengeful insensibility (for we must not neglect to mention here the ideal dandy type); sometimes too – and this is one of the most fascinating characteristics of Beauty – an element of mystery; and lastly (so as not to conceal the modernity of my aesthetics), an element of *unhappiness*. I do not claim that Joy is utterly foreign to Beauty, but I do maintain that it is one of Beauty's most commonplace, trivial ornaments, whereas Melancholy is, so to speak, her illustrious companion, and so closely linked to her that I can scarcely conceive (or is my brain a bewitched mirror?) of a type of Beauty where Unhappiness is absent. Resting on (others would say: obsessed with) these ideas, it is easy to understand why it would be difficult for me not to conclude that the perfect ideal of virile masculine Beauty is Satan, as Milton portrayed him.

BAUDELAIRE TO THEOPHILE GAUTIER: "I HAVEN'T A PENNY"
The words coming from Baudelaire's lips in this drawing of his (1857-58) indicate rather clearly that life itself had belied the statements he had made in 1846.

Ch. Baudelaire

THE SUBLIME ART OF ACTING

Like the toy and the picture-book, the theatre is often one of the child's first intimations of Beauty. In his prose-poem entitled *Vocations,* Baudelaire puts the following words into the mouth of a little boy:

> Yesterday my parents took me to the theatre. In grand and sorrowful palaces, behind which you can see the sky and the sea, men and women, serious and sorrowful too, but much more beautiful and finer dressed than any you have ever seen before, were talking in musical voices. They threatened each other, they pleaded, they wept, and often placed their hand against the dagger that is stuck in their belt. Oh, it's all very beautiful! The women are much prettier and taller than the ones that come to visit at your house, and, although they are sort of frightening with their big, deep-sunk eyes and their fiery cheeks, you can't help but fall in love with them anyway.... It's scary, you want to cry, and yet, somehow it makes you feel that you too would like to be dressed up just like them, the actors, and do the same sort of things, speak with the same sort of voice....

This enchantment, which he himself succumbed to as a child, furnished Baudelaire with one of his most frequent themes:

> It would not be surprising, he wrote in his *Morale du Joujou,* if a child, whose parents had given him miniature theatres to play with so that he could prolong the pleasure that he had received from live and marionette performances, should soon come to consider the theatre as the most delightful form of beauty.

In *My Heart Laid Bare,* he notes:

93

As a child, I sometimes wanted to be a Pope – but a warrior Pope – and sometimes an actor.

Joys that I extracted from these two day-dreams.

It comes as something of a surprise that in his journals he chose to recognize only three "respectable professions: priest, soldier, and poet" and did not see fit to elevate the actor to the same dignity. However, in his *Salon of 1859* he storms against those who commit the "sacrilege" of insulting the "sublime art of acting," and in his essay on Guys, written toward the end of the same year, he says of the actress that "if one side of her nature reveals the courtesan, the other contains the poet" – a statement which, coming from Baudelaire, can only be considered a genuine compliment.

In *Fanfarlo* where, as we have already remarked, he lends some of his own traits to the poet Samuel Cramer, Baudelaire emphasizes his hero's extraordinary gift for mimicry and self-deception; that is to say, his ability to adopt and act out a role:

One of Samuel's most characteristic peculiarities was his habit of equating himself to anyone who managed to acquire his admiration; after having passionately devoured a beautiful book, his involuntary conclusion was invariably: here is something fine enough to be my own work! – and from there flowed the thought: *ergo,* it must be my own work. Only the short span of a dash separated the two thoughts.

Every inch a gentleman by birth, and something of a scoundrel by preference – an actor by temperament – he performed for his own pleasure, and in the privacy of his own rooms, grandiose tragedies, or perhaps one should say, tragi-comedies. If he felt himself touched, or ever so slightly tickled, by a sensation of merriment, he thought himself compelled to verify the sensation and set about producing great bursts of laughter. If some tender memory caused a tear to well up in the corner of his eye, he hastened to the mirror to watch himself weep. If one of his more hot-tempered mistresses, in a fit of violent and puerile jealousy, scratched him with a knitting-needle or her tiny pen-knife, Samuel glorified in this saber wound. And when he found himself owing a paltry twenty-thousand francs to some creditor, he would cry out in exaltation: How sad and woeful is the fate of a genius plagued by a million in debts!

But mind that you do not conclude from this that he was incapable of experiencing genuine sentiments as well, and that, for him, passion was nothing more than a passing fancy. He had in the past sold his shirts to help a man whom he scarcely knew and whom he had, just the day before, accepted as an intimate friend after a brief examination of his forehead and hands. . . . He had fought a duel to defend the honor of some author or painter dead for over two centuries. As he had formerly been a fervent example of piety, so was he today the most passionate of atheists. He was at one and the same time all the books that he had ever read and all the artists that he had ever studied; and yet, in spite of this penchant for play-acting, he managed to preserve intact his own profound originality. He was always the same sweet, outlandish, lazy, frightening, scholarly, uninformed, slovenly, foppish Samuel Cramer. . . . He would dote on a friend as he would on a woman, and treat a woman with the same respect as a friend. He grasped the logic of all noble sentiments and the science of all underhanded tricks, and yet, he never succeeded in anything because he believed too strongly in the impossible. And how can we find that surprising? He was always busy bringing it into being.

Cramer's strange solitary performances recall the lines of Poe that Baudelaire quotes in his article on the actor Rouvière, and which, as he says, make him pause "to dream over the artistry of great actors": "When I wish to ascertain to what degree some person is circumspect or stupid, to what degree he is good or evil, or to discover what he is thinking about at any given moment, I model my features as closely as possible on his and then wait to see what thoughts or sentiments enter brain or heart, as though they were seeking to fit into and correspond with my new physiognomy."

The conclusion of this same article gives us an idea of the sort of intellectual fulfilment, that Baudelaire would have found on the stage, if fate had complied with his childhood dreams and made him an actor:

When the great actor, costumed and painted, impregnated with his role, finds himself in front of a mirror and there contemplates this new personality – terrifying or charming, seductive or repulsive – which must supplant his own for the next few hours, he acquires from this analysis a unique feeling of fulfilment, a sort of recurrent self-hypnosis. Then the magic operation is over, the miracle of total objectivity accomplished, and the artist can utter his *Eureka*. The personification of love or hatred, he can then step on to the stage.

ONLY TRUE IN ANOTHER WORLD

Although he has left us lengthy critical studies on the painting of Delacroix, the drawings of Guys, and the music of Wagner, Baudelaire seems to reveal a strange reluctance to discuss his own work. On examining the draft for an unpublished preface to the second or third edition of the *Fleurs du Mal*, we find that he has avoided any confidences and given himself up to somewhat caustic clowning. For example:

> Given: that poetry is related to the arts of painting, cooking, and cosmetics through its ability to express all the sensations of sweetness or bitterness, beatitude or horror by the coupling of a certain substantive with a certain adjective, analogous or contradictory.
>
> It follows that: by heeding my principles and employing the knowledge that I will undertake to impart to him in twenty easy lessons, any man who so chooses will be able to turn out a tragedy which will be no worse than the others, or put together a poem of sufficient length to be every bit as boring as any known piece of epic poetry.

Although he was hesitant about discussing his work before the public, in the privacy of his notebooks or correspondence he was considerably more expansive. In a notation that dates from 1855 he has recorded this very broad, but nonetheless highly personal definition of poetry:

> Poetry is that which is the most real, that which is entirely true only in *another world*.

In a letter to the critic Armand Fraisse, Baudelaire begins by congratulating the journalist for his favorable comments on the sonnets of Soulary and then continues on into a lengthy eulogy of the sonnet itself – less perhaps out of any marked preference for that particular form than out of a distinct dislike for the weighty, but fashionable, alexandrine line which all too often tended to tumble into redundance and mere verbiage. He himself had tried his hand with the alexandrine, and not without a certain amount of success, but he never felt at ease in its rambling expanses. The sonnet was more to his taste: "Because the form is restrictive, the idea spurts forth with more vigor." The letter continues:

> The sonnet is hospitable to all sorts of subject matter: buffoonery, gentle wooing, passion, reverie, philosophical reflection. It has the beauty of a highly polished metal or gem. Have you ever noticed that a fragment of the heavens, perceived through a port-hole, or between two chimney-pots, two rocks, or through an arcade, etc., leaves you with a more profound idea of infinity than a grand panorama viewed from the heights of a mountain? As for long poems, we know what we think about them; they are the last resort of poets who are incapable of writing short ones.
>
> Anything that exceeds in duration the amount of attention a human being can apply to a poetic form, is not *a poem*. (Letter of February 18, 1860.)

The various drafts that we possess of some of Baudelaire's completed poems tell us of the patient, and even painful, labor that he imposed on himself during the process of composition. Baudelaire was not one of the Muse's spoiled darlings. Barrès could say of him, not without a certain amount of justice, that "he put magnificent prose into difficult verse." Whenever a particularly good line sang in his head he hastened to jot it down somewhere:

> *Tu m'as donné ta boue et j'en ai fait de l'or*

but he did not always succeed in building a poem around these isolated fragments of inspiration. He wrestled like a demon with rhyme and meter and occasionally had to resort to tautology (notably in the first stanza of the *Serpent qui danse*), in order to gain a somewhat Pyrrhic victory. But all that is of little consequence when we compare Baudelaire's poems to the empty productions of such able rhymsters as Banville and Gautier.

Constantly on the run from creditors who pursued him from one Paris hotel to another, he occasionally succumbed to fits of impotent rage:

> And to make matters all the more ridiculous, I am compelled, amidst all these unbearable calamities that leave me totally exhausted, to write verses – the most tiring of occupations for me. (Letter to his mother, April 5, 1855.)

In May, 1857 he wrote to his friend and publisher Poulet-Malassis, who was pressing him for the corrected proofs of the *Fleurs du Mal:*

> I am fighting with some thirty unsatisfactory lines – nasty lines, badly written, badly rhymed. Do you think that I have the facility of a Banville?

Inspiration, he said, visited him only on very rare occasions. Four months after the condemnation of the *Fleurs du Mal* he wrote to Malassis:

> You know that I have decided to submit whole-heartedly to the judgment and to write six new poems, much more beautiful than the suppressed ones. But when will I ever be able to recapture the necessary mood to write poetry? (Letter of December 30, 1857.)

Yet even when he has at last succeeded in recapturing the mood, he becomes suspicious of his inspiration. In June, 1859 he sent to Jean Morel, editor of the *Revue Française,* a poem entitled "Fantômes parisiens," and joined to this offering a most unenthusiastic commentary:

> All that I can say about the poem is that the effort it has cost me is no just indication of its merit; it is the first of a new series that I want to try to write, and I fear that I have simply succeeded in going beyond the limits assigned to Poetry.

He had so little confidence in the quality of the *Fantôme* cycle that, in spite of the time and energy he had already given to them, he rewrote the poems entirely before allowing them to be included in the second edition of the *Fleurs du Mal* under the title of the *Sept Vieillards*.

On the other hand, Baudelaire was prompt to spring to his own defense when Alphonse Calonne, the editor of the *Revue Contemporaine*, suggested that he make certain corrections on two poems ("L'amour du mensonge," and "Rêve parisien") that the poet had submitted for publication:

> Alas! your criticisms fall on just those very words, twists, and characteristics that I consider to be my strongest points.

And after having justified at length the choice and placement of his words, and the coherence of his metaphors, he adds:

> Those lines, I assure you, have been very painstakingly put together.

But such self-assurance was far from habitual with Baudelaire. For every poem that he considered finished, how many there were that never succeeded in satisfying him! At the same moment that he was rejecting the criticisms of Calonne, he wrote to Malassis that the twenty-five new poems that he had already submitted for the second edition of the *Fleurs du Mal* fell short of his expectations:

> I have just finished re-reading those twenty-five new pieces; there are still some heavy-handed passages, some jolts in the style. . . . What is your opinion of the last two tercets of the first sonnet of *Un fantôme?*

But if Baudelaire was a severe self-critic, if he accepted and sometimes solicited comments on his work from editors and publishers, he would never allow his texts to be altered by any hand save his own. Criticism, yes – censorship, never. He makes his attitude very clear in a letter that he wrote to Gervais Charpentier, editor of the *Revue Nationale*, who had accepted two of his short prose-poems:

Monsieur, I have just finished reading the two pieces of mine ("Les Tentations" and "Dorothée") published in the *Revue Nationale*. I came across some extraordinary changes made in the texts after I had submitted my final proofs. That, monsieur, is exactly the reason why I do my best to avoid publishing in newspapers and periodicals.

I have said to you before: throw out the *whole piece* if a *single comma* annoys you, but do not throw out the comma; it has a reason for being there.

I have spent my entire life learning how to construct sentences and I say to you, without fear of being ridiculous, that what I choose to turn over to the printer is *complete* down to the smallest detail.

Do you really believe that "the forms of her body" is equivalent to "her hollowed back and pointed breasts"? Especially when it has to do with a Negress from Western Africa?

And do you think that it is *immoral* to say that a girl is "ripe at eleven" when it is well known that Aïscha (who did not happen to be a Negress from the tropics) was even younger than that when she wed Mohammed?

Monsieur, I want, with all sincerity, to thank you for the kind reception your review has given me; but *I know what I mean when I write something* and I write only about things that *I have seen with my own eyes*.

If I had been warned in time I would have had the whole piece withdrawn. (Letter of June 20, 1863.)

To speak the truth, this very pertinent letter does contain one rather boastful mis-statement – for although it is a fact that Baudelaire never submitted any slipshod work to a printer, it is untrue to say that he ever considered anything he wrote completely satisfactory. Until receiving the final proofsheets, and even after he had sent them off, he hesitated, deliberated and rewrote. Every new edition was an opportunity for rewriting. Nothing, or almost nothing, that flowed from his pen seemed to him to be truly *finished*. Baudelaire was Sisyphus turned author.

On the other hand, as hastily written as the letter seems to be – it appears that he wrote it in one angry breath – there is nothing exaggerated about Baudelaire's final remarks. When he states that he knows what he is writing about, he is only claiming his lawful rights. This he knew for certain, for whatever subject he dealt with was drawn from his own experience, or – and here we are thinking of the influence of Poe – was assimilated by some sort of systematic and mystic transfusion.

When, in 1855, Fernand Desnoyers solicited his contribution to a collection of poems devoted to the palace of Fontainebleau and its forests, Baudelaire was able to offer him nothing but verses of a highly personal, and definitely urban, inspiration. Indeed, except for a few poems with exotic settings, Nature plays a very minor role in Baudelaire's work. He was indifferent to pastoral poetry and did not hesitate to say as much to his correspondent:

My dear Desnoyers, you are asking me for several lines on Nature, on woods, giant oaks, lawns, insects, and sunbeams – that's it; isn't it? Yet you know perfectly well that I am incapable of being sentimental over vegetables, and that my soul rebels against this strange new religion which, as far as I am concerned, will always have, for any *spiritual* person, something downright *shocking* about it. I will never bring myself to believe that *the soul of the Gods inhabits plants,* and even if it did dwell there, I would not give a rap about such a soul and would consider my own as being worth a good deal more than the soul of a sanctified vegetable. I have always thought that there was something painful and immodest in this *Nature* of yours, that blossoms and renews itself every year. Finding it impossible to satisfy you by following your requirements to the letter, I am nonetheless sending you two poems ("Le Crépuscule du matin" and "Le Crépuscule du soir") which give you some sort of idea of the mood that seizes twilight. In the depths of a forest, enveloped by arches that resemble those of a sacristy or cathedral, I think of our astonishing cities, and the mysterious music that reaches me from the hill-tops seems to be the translation of mankind's lamentations.

We have heard Baudelaire maintain that Beauty is by its very nature strange; that there can be no work of art that is devoid of a certain element of surprise. His own poetry adheres to this principle. If the word "scandalous" is employed in its strict etymological sense, it can be said that Baudelaire deliberately wrote scandalous poetry; that is to say, poetry that was intended to provoke surprise.

In 1852 he wrote to Théophile Gautier, whom he was counting on to help him place some of his future "fleurs du mal" in the *Revue de Paris*:

> Stick by me. If the public doesn't put up too much of a kick, I'll give them some more poems, even more *clairvoyant* than the last ones.

Clairvoyant poetry: the same term flows from his pen in a letter to Malassis, regarding his *Fleurs du Mal* which was just about to be turned over to the printer:

> We must have a volume made up only of good things: little bulk, with a great deal of content, and very *clairvoyant*. (December 9, 1856.)

And this same concern enters into the composition of the poems intended to enrich the second edition of the *Fleurs du Mal*:

> I am at work on the *Fleurs du Mal*. In a few days you will receive your parcel, and the last piece, or epilogue, addressed to the city of Paris, will perhaps startle you, if I ever succeed in whipping it into shape (with booming tercets). (Letter to Malassis, June, 1860.)

As we know, Baudelaire was destined never to finish this epilogue.

Bon à tirer.
Ch. Baudelaire

Quand la pluie étalant ses immenses traînées
D'une vaste prison imite les barreaux,
Et qu'un peuple muet d'horribles araignées
Vient tendre ses filets au fond de nos cerveaux,

(lancent)

Des cloches tout-à-coup sautent avec furie — *18*
Et ~~poussent~~ vers le ciel un ~~long gémissement,~~
Ainsi que des esprits errants et sans patrie
Qui se mettent à geindre opiniâtrément.

d'anciens

— Et ~~de grands~~ corbillards, sans tambour ni musique,
~~Passent~~ en foule au fond de mon âme ; et l'Espoir
Fuyant vers d'autres cieux, l'Angoisse despotique
Sur mon crâne incliné plante son drapeau noir.

défilent
lentement
dans

pleurant
Comme un
vaincu

15

(mettriez vous ici une virgule vu la construction de la phrase ?)

Je viens de faire une découverte affligeante. En comptant 2 pages pour les sonnets, 1 ½ strophes de 4 vers par page, cinq strophes de cinq vers, sept ou 8 strophes de 3 vers, 10 ou 12 strophes de deux vers, en supposant toujours deux strophes au dessous du titre, et deux pages pour les titres généraux, nous tomberons juste sur 240 pages. 10 feuilles. — La table des matières, tirée à part fera 5 pages au plus. — 245. — pitié, trois pitiés. — Et il n'y a pas de remède. Car si je ne me souciais pas de faire des vers nouveaux, et les sonnets par la Mort font une excellante conclusion — Il serait bon que ces trois feuilles dernières pussent finir le 10. May car j'ai fort soin pour la Table, et les Couvertures de la brochure. Si j'ajoutais un morceau des fleurs du mal, deux des sonnets par la Mort seraient rejetés dans la dernière feuille ou le carton final, et seraient tirés avec la table. — Dans une heure, je vais vous mettre à la poste les matières de votre 8e feuille, vous vous êtes obstiné à votre pluralité. — Il y a des Bonailles Beaumes pour Baumes. Je ne peux plus le retrouver, mais j'en suis sûr. —

BE ALWAYS A POET

Baudelaire's constant devotion to his lofty ideal of poetry explains why he never produced, in spite of years of labor, more than a single volume of poems. As was the case with Mallarmé, Baudelaire was paralyzed by his desire for perfection.

From the very beginning of his literary career, he regarded poetry as the quintessence of all the arts. He was scarcely twenty-five when he wrote, in February, 1846, the following passage in his *Advice to Young Writers*:

As for those who are devoting themselves, or have already devoted themselves with some success - to poetry, I advise them never to abandon it. Poetry is one of the arts that has the most to offer, but it is a long-term investment which yields interest only after many years – and then the returns are great.

I defy envious authors to name me the publisher who was ever ruined by good verse.

From the point of view of ethics, poetry makes such a very sharp distinction between first-raters and second-raters that even the most bourgeois readers are made aware of this despotic influence. I know several people who read the newspaper articles of Théophile Gautier only because he is the author of the *Comédie de la Mort*; doubtless they do not appreciate the full merit of this poem, but they do sense the presence of a real poet.

And what is so astonishing about this, since any man in reasonably good health can go without food for two days – but without poetry? Never!

The art which satisfies our most urgent need will always be the most highly honored.

Experience will take it upon itself to dissipate this illusion. Baudelaire, finally cornered by death, will cry out in 1866: "France has a horror of real poetry." The investment that he placed in his as yet unpublished verse in 1846 was one day to bring high dividends, but too late for him enjoy them; it was the publisher Michel Lévy who saw the stock mounting and who managed to reap the profit.

Although his opinion of the public was to undergo a change, he always remained faithful to his deep reverence for poetry . In *My Heart Laid Bare,* after twenty years of disappointments had brought him to the brink of utter dispair, he could still write:

> The only really great men are the poet, the priest, and the soldier.
> The man who sings, the man who blesses, the man who at the same time performs the sacrifice and offers himself for sacrifice.
> Be always a poet, even in prose.

"Be always a poet" – no mean task, for Baudelaire conceived of poetry as something lofty and universal, a conception that can perhaps be grasped today, but which could scarcely be understood over a hundred years ago. On the eve of the trial of the *Fleurs du Mal* Sainte-Beuve counseled Baudelaire to build his defense around the proposition that "poetry had exhausted its supply of subject matter," that Lamartine had taken out a patent on the heavens, Hugo, on the Earth (and a bit more, as well), Laprade, on the forests, Musset, on the passions, Gautier, on Spain and its "local color," other poets, on domestic bliss, rural life, etc., and that Baudelaire had been thus forced by circumstances to make use of the only material left over. This line of argument could scarcely be expected to carry much weight from a judicial point of view, but Sainte-Beuve probably suggested it, with a cynical shrug of the shoulders, in the belief that it might satisfy the lackadaisical logic of the public, which seemed to be determined that every artist should have his *genre.*

As for Baudelaire, he felt that there was absolutely no limit to the subjects that a great artist, poet or painter, could handle. He makes this point clear in his short study on Hugo:

> He who is not capable of engulfing everything in his

THEOPHILE GAUTIER *(Cabinet des Estampes)*.

works, palaces and hovels, compassion and cruelty, the integrated affections of family circles and sentiments of universal charity, the grace of plants and the miracles of architecture, everything that is soft and consoling, everything that fills the heart with dread, the intimate revelations and exterior beauty of each and every religion, the physical and moral composition of individual nations, in short, everything, from the visible to the invisible, from the heights of Heaven to the depths of Hell, he who is not capable of expressing all this is, in my judgment, not a true poet in the immense meaning of the word, in the meaning God gave to it. You say of one man, he is the poet of the *hearth,* or of the family; of another, he is the poet of love, and yet another, the poet of glory. But what right have you to limit the range of an artist's talents? Are you trying to maintain that he who has sung of glory is, *by that fact alone,* incapable of writing about love? By such reasoning you cripple the word *poetry* and deprive it of its true significance. If you simply mean by such a statement that certain circumstances, for which the poet can not be held responsible, have *up until now* limited him to one particular source of subject matter, I will naturally assume that you are referring to a minor poet, an under-developed poet, no matter how skilful he may be in his own *genre.*

These pencil-drawings apparently date from 1857, the same year that the Flowers of Evil appeared in print. The Goncourt brothers noted in their Journal: "Baudelaire at supper at the next table from us tonight. Goes about with no tie, an open collar, and his head shaved—exactly the costume of a man sent to the guillotine. A deliberate pretentiousness, in short: hands washed, scrubbed, and carefully manicured, like a woman's hands. And also the look of a maniac, a voice cutting as a voice of steel, and a studied turn of phrase that aims at the ornate precision of a Saint-Just and more than hits the mark."

A STRANGE WARNING

One can scarcely accuse the author of the *Fleurs du Mal* of having a narrow outlook on life. Although he has left us but a single volume of poems, it would be impossible in a study of this size to examine in detail all the various themes touched upon in this volume. In contrast to second-rank poets, who attempt to give each of their works a certain unity by carefully limiting their own emotional and philosophical range, Baudelaire's personality clearly emerges from a startling number of disparate elements. The harmony of the *Fleurs du Mal* lies not in its deliberate "well-roundedness" but rather in its fidelity to the poet's inner nature: it is, in sum, a confidential journal of an exceptionally sensitive being, a being condemned to cultivate his sensitivity, even at the cost of his own life. Sainte-Beuve, who did not seem to appreciate the full value of the *Fleurs du Mal*, did, however, grasp something of its essence when he wrote to its author, "You must have gone through great suffering, my poor boy."

Every poem of Baudelaire's has been tempered in the fire of this suffering, even when the poet attempts to disguise this fact. Some diligent reader has ascertained that the image of the *abyss* recurs eighteen times in the volume, as though the poet had had some strange premonition of the awful dizzy spells that were to seize him a few years later in Brussels, causing him to stagger like a drunkard, to cling frantically to the furniture of his hotel room. All devoted Baudelaire readers know by heart the prophetic passage of *My Heart Laid Bare* where, five years before his death, he evokes his final collapse:

Morally as well as physically, I have always carried with me the sensation of an abyss, not only the abyss of sleep, but of action too, of dreams, memories, desires, longings, beauty, numbers, etc. . . .

I have cultivated my hysteria with terror and delight. Now I am always on the verge of fainting, and today, January 23, 1862, I have had a strange warning, I have felt the wings of madness hovering over me.

This "strange warning" was probably the culmination of a series of signals. Perhaps it had come to him shortly after he had written his sonnet entitled "The Abyss"; in any case, his poem on "The Taste for Oblivion" had already appeared in print some three years before:

LE GOUT DE NÉANT

Dull soul, once fond of conflict and dispute,
Hope, whose spur might prick you on again,
will straddle you no more. Rest without shame,
old horse stumbling on every stone and root.

Resign yourself, my heart. Sleep like a brute.

Broken, foundered scoundrel, it is your doom:
love has no more relish, nor the struggle.
Farewell, then, sighing flute and singing bugle!
Pleasures, tempt no more my heart's dark gloom!

Spring, adorable season, has lost its perfume!

As a body stiffens in the snow's thick pall,
minute by minute Time is engulfing me.
I gaze from the heights at the earth's rotundity
and I seek no shelter there, however small.

Avalanche, will you take me in your fall?
(Translated by C. F. MacIntyre)

LE GOUFFRE

Pascal had his abyss, which moved with him,
– alas, all is but void – act, dream, desire,
word! and often my bristling hair and skin
feel the passage of the wings of Fear.

Above, below, around, on sea or strand,
in silence, and enticing frightful space . . .
in my nights' depths, God with his clever hand
sketches a nightmare, multiform, no truce,

I'm afraid of sleep as one fears an abyss,
full of vague horror, leading none knows where;
my windows show me but infinities;

haunted by vertigo, my spirit despairs,
envious of unconscious Nothingness.
– Ah, never to leave Numbers and Entities!
(Translated by C. F. MacIntyre)

Grand ange qui portez sur votre fier visage
La noirceur de l'Enfer d'où vous êtes monté;
Dompteur froid et doux qui m'avez mis en rage
Pour servir de Spectacle à votre [ ] éventé,

Cauchemar de my Nuits, Sirène sans corsage,
qui me tirez toujours, Debout à mon côté,
Par ma robe de Saint ou une broste de Sage
Pour m'offrir le poison d'un amour [ ];
. . . .

I FLEE FROM SLEEP

Baudelaire's statement that "I write only about what I have seen" begins, at this stage of his life, to assume tragic dimensions. For him, the familiar theme of "wingèd Time" is not a cliché, the Lamartinian exercises of a robust poet who can look forward to a long and vigorous existence. Time haunted his most intimate utterances, and we frequently come across this fearful specter in his journals. From *Fusées*:

> By count, I am thirty years old; and yet, if I have actually lived three minutes in one ... does that not make me ninety?

And indeed, at Brussels, in his forty-fifth year, his head was crowned with flowing white hair and he could have been easily mistaken for an old man.

In a prose-poem from *Le Spleen de Paris*, it is Time that haunts the "Double Room":

> ... In this narrow world, so overcrowded with disgusting objects, there is only one thing that can bring a smile to my lips: a phial of laudanum. My old and terrible friend; and like all friends, alas!, overflowing with caresses and betrayals.
>
> Yes, oh yes! Time has returned from exile; he reigns supreme now. And the hideous old creature has brought with him his entire demoniac entourage: Memories, Remorse, Spasms, Fears, Agonies, Nightmares, Angers, and Neuroses.
>
> I can assure you that each second is now loudly and solemnly announced, each swing of the pendulum proclaims: "I am Life, insufferable, implacable Life!"
>
> There is only a single second in human existence that bears us good news, *the* Good News, which every man holds in inexplicable dread.
>
> Yes! Time reigns; he has re-established his brutal dictatorship. And he prods me on with his double-pronged staff, as though I were an abject old cow.

113

Frontispiece for JETSAM (LES ÉPAVES), *by Rops.*

"Get along with you! Ho there! You bag of beef,
you slave! Get along with you and live, accursed
soul!"

The specter of Time haunts all his work, especially the
Fleurs du Mal. In "Moesta et errabunda":

How far away you seem, sweet scented paradise. . . .

in the "Ennemi":

– Agony! oh agony! Time devours my days,
And the dark enemy who gnaws at the heart
Grows great from the blood that streams from the
[wound.

and "l'Horloge":

Clock, sinister deity, impassive, frightening,
whose finger threatens us and says: *"Remember!*
soon come the quivering Sorrows to your somber
fearful heart as to a target winging;

"Pleasure fades away toward the horizon
like a sylph who disappears past the coulisse;
each instant eats from you a little piece
of pleasure granted all men in their season.

"Thirty-six hundred times an hour, each fast
Second whispers: *Mind, now!* – and its voice is
like an insect's; the Now says: I'm the Past,
I've sucked your life out with my foul proboscis!

"Souviens-toi! Remember! Esto memor!
(My metal throat can speak each foreign tongue.)
The minutes, wanton mortal, are the ore
whence you must leave no bit of gold unwrung!

"Remember that Time is a voracious gambler
who wins – it is the law – at every throw!
Day dwindles as night deepens – oh, *remember!*
the gulf thirsts and the clepsydra runs low.

"Soon strikes the hour when inexorable Fate,
when august Virtue, your still virgin wife,
when even Repentance (oh, last inn of life!),
will all say: Die, old coward! It's too late!"

(Translated by C. F. MacIntyre)

This obsession of Time, this anguish which gripped him so firmly that he frequently could not find the courage to open his mail, was to tarnish his existence, was to transform every object, every action, into a symbol of physical and moral decay. Baudelaire's poems teem with images of degeneration: devoured hearts, bloodless lips, toothless jaws, putrefying flesh, ravaged souls, running sores, cracked walls. Four poems of the *Fleurs du Mal* ("Une charogne," "Remords posthume," "Le Mort joyeux," "Le voyage a Cythère") contain descriptions of bodily decomposition. "La Cloche fêlée" reveals the poet's shattered spirit. "Le Jeu" and "Les Petites Vielles" conjure up the vision of disjointed monsters that "once were women." The imagery of "Une Martyre" is in the style of a Rops drawing, with the artist choosing as scenery the dissecting room of a medical school.

Even sleep could not free Baudelaire from his sense of doom. One morning, upon awakening, he noted in his journal the tortuous dreams of the past night:

Symbols of decay. Immense Pelasgian ruins, piled one upon the other. Apartments, chambers, *temples,* galleries, caecums, belvederes, lanterns, fountains, statues. – *Cracks,* crevices. Dampness, issuing from a *reservoir* situated near the sky. – How to warn the people? – Let's whisper a warning to the most intelligent.

High up, a column cracks, and its two extremities slip out of place. Nothing has collapsed as yet. I can't find the way out. I descend, then go up again. *A tower. – Labyrinth. I will never be able to escape. I will always inhabit this structure that is just about to crumble, a building undermined by some secret disease.* – To pass the time, I amuse myself by trying to calculate to what extent this enormous mass of stones, marbles, statues, walls, which are going to crash down one upon the other, will be stained by this multitude of brains, flesh, ground-up bones. I see such horrible things in my dreams that I sometimes feel that I want to evermore flee from sleep, if it were not for the fact that I dread the consequences of excessive fatigue.

POETRY HAS NO OTHER END BUT ITSELF

Baudelaire's works were twice hauled into the law courts on criminal charges. In August, 1857 the attorney for the State, Pinard, denounced the *Fleurs du Mal* as an attack on both public and religious morality, and the Sixth Correctional Chamber applauded his declaration by condemning the "injurious effect" of the book's imagery. Then in May, 1868, eight months after the poet's death, the criminal court of Lille ordered the destruction of Baudelaire's last publication, the slender volume of *Épaves,* brought out in Brussels by Poulet-Malassis, which contained the six poems condemned the year before. Whether in or out of the law courts, Baudelaire's work was almost universally damned by his contemporaries. As early as 1843, when he was only twenty-three years old and still entirely unknown as a writer, Baudelaire had to struggle against faint-hearted newspaper editors who, above all, had no intention of running the risk of offending their subscribers. These rejected articles were not, however, so offensive that they could not be shown to his mother:

> Please be good enough to read through this manuscript which, except for a little polishing, is entirely finished. I picked it up this morning at the office of *La Démocratie* where it was rejected on grounds of immorality. What's so very amusing about the whole affair is that they were so taken aback by the piece that they did me the honor of requesting a second one right then and there.

Twenty-one years later, in 1864, the young editor of *La Revue Libérale,* Edouard Le Boucher, accepted several of Baudelaire's prose-poems for publication and then saw fit to make a few "indispensable" alterations in

117

the texts. As he attempted to explain in a letter to his friend Taine, a sober-minded review could not tolerate the "sadistic methods" employed by a Flaubert or a Baudelaire.

Let it be stated, however, that Baudelaire never set out with the deliberate intention to offend public morality. Although he did not scorn the effects of surprise ("beauty is bizarre") he never had recourse to the condiments of licentious literature. Even his most passionate poems contain none of that gratuitous sensuality that belongs to the realm of pornography; Baudelaire had nothing but disgust and disdain for the highly spiced productions of the eighteenth century, as one of his letters to Poulet-Malassis, in which he requests some information for his friend Sainte-Beuve, clearly demonstrates:

> I would be very grateful if you would drop me a line, as soon as possible, telling me the price of a copy of *Justine* and where this book can be obtained, also, the price of *Aphrodites* and the *Diable au Corps,* and what you consider to be the moral or literary characteristics of the similar sort of garbage written by Mirabeau and Restif.
>
> And what the devil does Monsieur Baudelaire want with such filth? Monsieur Baudelaire has enough genius to study the evil that lurks in his own heart. This note is sent on behalf of a great man who believes that evil must be studied away from home.

But although Baudelaire had no intention of offending public morality, neither did he intend to be victimized by it. His ideas on the relationship between art and morals are clearly stated: the work of art is, by its very nature, moral because it stems from a yearning for beauty; the task of the poet and novelist is to write, not preach; they are creators, not magistrates. In his *Notes nouvelles sur Edgar Poe (Further notes on Edgar Poe),* published in 1857 (and which Baudelaire, for once satisfied with one of his works, thought important enough to reincorporate in his essay on Gautier), he denounces what he considers to be the heresy of artistic heresies: subjugating art to morality.

There is a great herd of people who believe that the aim of poetry is to teach some sort of lesson, that a poem ought to bolster the conscience, improve manners, in short, be of practical use in some way or other. Poetry (as little as people may want to descend into themselves, interrogate their own souls, recall the memories of their past enthusiasms) has no other aim but Itself; its nature forbids it having any other, and the only poem truly worthy of the title, Poem, is one that has been written solely for the pleasure of writing a poem.

I do not mean to say – please try to understand me – that poetry does not have a beneficial effect on society, that the final results of poetry do not serve to raise man above his usual vulgar concerns; such a statement would be absurd. What I do mean to say is that if a poet deliberately sets out to preach a moral he necessarily diminishes his poetic strength, and it would not be unwise to wager that the resulting poem will be a bad one. Poetry simply can not, under penalty of death or decay, become an appendage of science or morality. It's goal is not Truth, but only Itself. There are other means, other methods, by which truths may be perceived. Truth has nothing to do with songs. The very things that constitute the charm, the grace, the magic of a song strip Truth of its power and authority. Cold, calm, impassive, the demonstrational temperament repects the diamonds and flowers of the Muse; it is indeed, the very antithesis of the poetic temperament.

In fact, none of the various manifestations of art find their source of inspiration in morality. Nor is the novel a tributary of this same morality; Baudelaire, in his preface to the *Martyrs ridicules,* deplores the fact that Cladel has mutilated the narrative of his book by sermonizing:

In one of the best passages of the book, the author introduces us to a sympathetic sort of creature, an officer, lacking in neither honor nor intelligence, but old before his time, worn out by worries and the

119

treacherous effects of habitual drunkenness, who falls prey to the pranks of his barroom cronies. The reader is made aware of Pipab's former moral strength, and can he help but share this brave old veteran's martyrdom, as he watches him clowning, crawling, dancing, cajoling, in order to coax from his young tormentors . . . what? – A pitiful last glass of absinthe. Suddenly the author's indignation breaks forth from the mouth of one of his characters who expresses in vigorous terms his disapproval of the antics of these young rotters. The speech is very eloquent, very elevating; unfortunately the author's own voice, his naive indignation, is not well enough concealed. We catch sight of the writer lurking behind the scenery. The truly masterful touch would have been for him to have remained cool and aloof, and to bequeath to the reader this meritorious indignation. The effect of this horrible scene would have been intensified. That public morality here receives its pittance, that is incontestable; but art suffers, and with true art, true morality. To present the case skillfully is always sufficient.

Flaubert, an artist of quite another class than Cladel, took care never to weigh down his tale of Mme Bovary with moral digressions. Baudelaire, naturally enough, was quick to appreciate the novelist's viewpoint, and very shortly after the condemnation of his own *Fleurs du Mal* wrote an article in the *Artiste* praising *Madame Bovary:*

Several critics have said: this work, undeniably fine in the detail and vivacity of its descriptive passages, does not contain a single character who represents morality, who acts as spokesman for the author's conscience. Where is he hiding, this legendary and proverbial character whose job it is to superintend the reader's intelligence? In other words, where is our attorney for the prosecution?

And what nonsense this is! The eternal and incorrigible confusion concerning the functions and methods of art! A true work of art has no need of an attorney. The logic of the work satisfies all the postulates of morality, and it is the reader's task to draw the conclusions from the conclusion.

We must not be led to believe that the above principles were born of the necessity to defend his own poetry against the accusations that were then being hurled at it by the public. As early as 1851 he professed the same convictions in an article on "Les Drames et les Romans hônnetes." Here the immediate object of attack is the inept School of Common Sense playwrights, led by Ponsard and Augier:

There are several words, terrifying and statuesque, that find their way into every literary polemic: art, beauty, utility, morality. A great free-for-all ensues, and for lack of philosophical assurance, each combatant grabs hold of part of the banner, proclaiming that the other portion has no value.... It is sad to note that we come across similar errors in two opposing schools: the bourgeois school and the socialist school. Both of them cry out together with missionary fervor: Listen to the moral! Listen to the moral! Naturally enough, one preaches bourgeois morality, the other socialist morality. Art becomes nothing more than propaganda.

Is art utilitarian? Yes. Why? Because it is art. Can art ever be pernicious? Yes. The sort of art that defies the basis of life. Vice is seductive and must be painted as seductive; but it brings with it its own sicknesses and pains, and they too must be described. If you set about to study these diseases like a young interne in a hospital, the School of Common Sense, that exclusively moralistic school, will find no way to batter down your defenses. Is crime always punished, virtue always rewarded? No, and yet, if your novel, if your play is well written it will never encourage anyone to violate the laws of nature. The prerequisite for healthy art is a belief in an integral unity. I defy anyone to find me a work of imagination that fulfills all the necessary conditions of beauty and which can be labelled as pernicious.

... I have a friend who for several years trumpeted the name of Berquin into my ears. Now there's a real writer! Berquin, a charming, good-natured, compassionate, benevolent author – a great author! Having had as a child the good, or perhaps bad, fortune to have read only adult literature, I was not acquainted with the works of this Berquin. One day when my brain was utterly befogged by the fashionable quandary of Art and Morality, the guardian angel of writers placed a volume of Berquin within my reach. At first glance I come across children who speak like grownups, like books, and who preach at their parents. Here, I say to myself, is false art. As I read on, what do I find but goodness constantly being rewarded with lollypops and wickedness invariably made ridiculous by inevitable punishment. If you behave yourself you will get a *yum-yum* – that is the whole basis of this sort of morality. Virtue becomes the *sine qua non* of success. It is enough to make one wonder whether Berquin was actually a Christian. Here without a doubt, I say to myself, is pernicious art, for the disciple of Berquin, on entering into the world, will lose no time in adopting the reciprocal formula: success is the condition *sine qua non* of virtue. Moreover, nourished on the teachings of his worthy tutor, he will be utterly deceived by the smiling face of prosperous crime and will make himself at home in a brothel, believing himself to be lodged in the mansion of high morals.

The same principles prompted Baudelaire's attitude toward official awards. The article from which we have just quoted above ("Les Drames et les Romans hônnetes"), published several days before the "coup d'état" of December 2, 1851, contains a polemic against a recent decree by which the minister Faucher established a series of prizes to be awarded to works of the theatre "that serve to instruct and enlighten the working-classes by the propagation of healthy ideas and by the representation of noble actions." Baudelaire answered:

Prizes bring misfortune. Academic prizes, prizes for Virtue, decorations, all those diabolical inventions that encourage hypocrisy and paralyze the spontaneous gestures of a generous heart. When I hear of a man applying to his sovereign for a medal, words something like this pass through my mind: I have done my duty, Sire, and no man can deny the fact, but if you do not proclaim this to the world, I swear that I will not continue to do it. . . .

What is to prevent a couple of scoundrels putting their heads together in order to carry off the Prix Montyon? One of them will play the beggar and the other will play the good Samaritan. There is something about official prize-giving that degrades both man and humanity, that offends both modesty and virtue. As far as I am concerned, I want nothing to do with a man who has won a prize for virtue: I would be afraid of finding myself in the clutches of an implacable tyrant.

As for writers, their prize is the esteem of their equals and the royalties from their publishers.

What the devil has Monsieur le Ministre to do with all of this? Does he want to engender hypocrisy so that he can have the pleasure of awarding it one of his prizes? Now we will see our boulevards turned into the stage-set for an interminable sermon. When an author finds himself with several months' rent overdue, he sits down and dashes off an "elevating" play; if his debts keep mounting, an "angelic" dream will be called for. A lovely institution, Monsieur le Ministre!

The rewards offered for "useful" art irritated Baudelaire, and with him, all the advanced thinkers of his day, but met with no opposition from the bourgeoisie and the socialists, both of whom based their existence on the framework of morality – and ultimately became the tools of the police state. In *My Heart Laid Bare* Baudelaire wrote:

All those idiots of the bourgeoisie who persist in muttering about "immoral art, immorality in art, morality in art" and similar idiotic phrases, make me think of Louise Villedieu, a two-penny whore who accompanied me one day to the Louvre, which she had never before visited, and then began to blush and to hide her face, all the while tugging me by the sleeve and inquiring, in front of all those immortal paintings and statues, how one could ever dare display before the public such horrid filth.

123

THE RED RIBBON AND THE ACADEMY

By a malicious prank of fate, Baudelaire, the scorner of official honors, was one day to submit his candidature for the French Academy and gaze longingly at the Légion d'honneur. The onslaught of ill-fortune made it almost impossible for him to stand to the defense of his cherished principles; the condemnation of the *Fleurs du Mal* and subsequent inability to earn a living by his writing compelled this humiliating surrender. Basically, his ideas had not changed but his financial situation had become desperate.

The ever-increasing poverty of her thirty-five-year-old son quite convinced Mme Aupick that she had taken the proper step in placing the poet's inheritance in the hands of an attorney in spite of the youth's repeated protestations. And now Baudelaire knew that some sort of public recognition – a red ribbon first, and in due time, a seat in the Academy – would be needed to convince her that her son was not a total failure from whom nothing but worry and unhappiness could be expected.

On August 22, 1858, he wrote her:

> The fifteenth of August has come and gone, and no decoration. I do not recall whether I ever mentioned to you that I had a chance for one last year as well but that the condemnation of the *Fleurs du Mal* postponed the issue until a future date. All the same, to speak with complete frankness, I found the recent nominations so utterly unspeakable that I am delighted at not having been tossed into the stew, especially that stew.

"That stew" was, in fact, no better nor worse than the others. Murger was awarded a bit of red ribbon and Sandeau a rosette. Such distinctions should scarcely have aroused either the envy or indignation of Baudelaire who had written in his *My Heart Laid Bare:*

> If a man has any merit, what is the good of decorating him? If he has none, then go ahead with the decoration because that will give him a little luster.
>
> To consent to be decorated is to acknowledge that the State or the Prince has the right to judge you, to make you illustrious, etc.

Later, in 1860, he again wrote to his mother on this subject:

> Once again it is a question of that ridiculous Légion d'honneur. I trust that my new preface to the *Fleurs* will bring a conclusive end to such prospects. Besides, I recently rebuffed one of my friends who offered to lend me some of his influence with the words: "Twenty years ago" (and I know what I'm saying is utter nonsense) "twenty years ago that would have been fine! Today I'd rather be the *exception.* Let them decorate every breathing Frenchman *except* me. I will never change either my behavior or my style of writing. Instead of a medal, let them give me *money, money,* nothing but money. If the medal is worth five hundred francs, let them give me the five hundred; if it is worth only twenty, I'll take that in cash." In short, I replied to those mutton-heads just like a *mutton-head.* The more miserable I become, the more my pride grows stronger. (Letter of October 11, 1860.)

But in spite of this scorn, which was certainly sincere, Baudelaire never ceased to yearn for some sort of decoration in order to wave it in the faces of his chief tormentors, the two or three ignorant bourgeois neighbors who constantly surrounded Mme Aupick – and in order to gain the precious respect and esteem of his mother.

His fantastic attempt to enter the French Academy, at the end of 1861, springs from the same desire. The Academy as a group seemed to impress him no more than the ranks of the Légionnaires. Except for Saint-Beuve and de Vigny (Hugo was then in exile), there were no academicians that he could look up to as his masters,

According to Jacques Crépet "the wide ribbon that adorns Baudelaire's button-hole allows us to determine the date of this drawing, for in the years 1857-1858, just before and just after the Flowers of Evil trial, Baudelaire entertained hopes of being decorated. As for the sack of gold crowns flying off on swift wings, we know that he never managed to catch it."

or even regard as his peers. In a letter written on December 11 to the secretary of the Academy in order to request the inclusion of his name on the list of candidates, Baudelaire concludes with the following words:

> The principal consideration that prompts me to solicit your suffrage is that, if I made up my mind to wait until I felt myself worthy to do so, I would never solicit it at all. I said to myself, after all, I might just as well take the step now; if my name is known to several among you, perhaps my audacity will be taken in good spirit, and several votes, *miraculously* obtained, would be considered by me as a generous gesture of encouragement and an order to do better in the future.

The truth seems to be clear enough: Baudelaire nourished no illusions concerning his chances of election; several "miraculous" votes would have contented him and would have demonstrated to his mother that several "eminent" men deigned to recognize her son's talents. In his state of physical and mental misery, such a testamonial would have been precious. He entered the ranks of candidates in the same spirit as a debtor, pursued by process-servers, purchases a lottery ticket which could win him a great amount of money – but not enough to save him. Several days before the election to fill the chair left empty by the death of Lacordaire, he accepted the advice of Sainte-Beuve and withdrew his name from the list of candidates. He would not have received a single vote. "Your withdrawal was not unfavorably received," Sainte-Beuve wrote him on February 15, 1862, "but when your final phrase of thanks was read aloud, conceived in such modest and polite terms, everyone cried out: Well done! Thus you have left behind you a very favorable impression, and isn't that something?

We shall leave Sainte-Beuve and his distinguished colleagues with their "favorable impression" of Monsieur Baudelaire. The noted critic scarcely understood the merits and importance of the *Fleurs du Mal,* but at least he was able to appreciate the courtesy, both innate and refined, of the poet to whom he feared to lend his patronage.

BAUDELAIRE AND THE GOVERNMENT

If Baudelaire was guilty of contradicting himself when he courted the Academy, he was also guilty of the same intellectual misdemeanor when he applied for government support.

In 1855 he could still boast that he had never sought favors from any public officials. Reporting a conversation that he had had with his legal guardian, he wrote to Mme Aupick:

I told Ancelle this morning something that I consider very sensible. I said to him: would you prefer that I follow the example of most men of letters, who have less pride than I do, and do what I have never done before under any ministry, under any government? The thought of asking a minister for money fills me with horror, and yet it has become practically an established custom; funds have been set aside to meet this demand. As for me, my pride and prudence have always prevented me from taking such a step. I will never allow my name to appear on a government payroll. I would rather be in debt to the whole world.

Two years later it was no longer possible for him to stand by his decision. Indeed, it now seemed that he was actually in debt to the whole world; in any case, he exhausted all his sources of credit. And the money owed him by various newspapers and reviews was often not forthcoming due to lack of funds. On the eve of the publication of the *Fleurs du Mal* he applied to the Minister of Public Instruction for assistance and his Excellency Gustave Rouland granted him, several days later, 200 francs from the fund "for the Encouragement of Science and the Arts."

After this initial success Baudelaire was on several occasions to seek government aid. In November, 1857, shortly after the condemnation of his book, he even addressed a letter to the Empress in order to obtain, if not a complete annulment, at least a reasonable reduction of the 300-franc fine that the court had imposed upon him. On January 20, 1858 the Keeper of the Seals did indeed reduce the fine to fifty francs, and the Minister of Public Instruction, by awarding him a second grant of 100 francs, more than compensated the impoverished poet for the immediate financial effects of the legal action.

Hugo's letter to Baudelaire has often been quoted to demonstrate that the unfortunate artist was one of the victims of the tyranny of the Second Empire. "What the regime chooses to call justice," wrote Hugo, "has condemned you in the name of what it likes to call morality." A resonant phrase, but far removed from the truth. The errors, even the crimes, of the Second Empire are well known to history, but Baudelaire can not be said to have suffered at the hands of the regime. His real persecutor was the bourgeoisie, the most narrow-minded and – in spite of their pious protestations – the least spiritually endowed elements of this bourgeoisie: those whose true Breviary was the gossip columns of the "accepted" newspapers. When the Public Prosecutor ranted, when the Sixth Chamber of the Criminal Courts issued its condemnation, the magistrates were not submitting to governmental directives, and were certainly not influenced by the opinion of the *Moniteur,* a quasi-official government-sponsored newspaper which published an article by Edouard Thierry in support of the much maligned book; no, they were simply echoing the judgment of the *Figaro,* the Bible of the bourgeoisie: "Nothing can justify a man of over thirty for having put before the public such a mass of monstrous obscenities." (*Le Figaro,* July 5, 1857).

And so it was that, during the period of his greatest distress and discouragement, in 1866, when Baudelaire was heaping abuse on almost everything and everybody, when France filled him with horror and Belgium (which he was then trying to escape from) with disgust, he never thought of turning his fury against the regime which Hugo credited with the condemnation of the *Fleurs du Mal.*

130

FRANCE HAS A HORROR OF POETRY

We have, in general, thought it best not to put too much emphasis on the very last writings of Baudelaire: his illness seems to have upset his equilibrium and prevented him from weighing his words with his customary care. However, at the beginning of this study we did quote several lines from a letter to Ancelle written in February, 1866 and we now wish to quote the entire passage: Baudelaire, by a passionate enumeration of his hates, gives us a revealing picture of his true affinities:

> You have been naive enough to overlook the fact that France has a horror of poetry, of real poetry; she cares only for swine like Musset and Béranger; whoever fusses over his spelling passes for a heartless creature (which is not entirely without some logic since passion is always badly expressed in words); in short, poetry that is profound, but complex, bitter, coldly diabolical (in appearance) is less fit for those eternally frivolous minds than any other sort!
>
> Must I explain to you, you who seem to have guessed no more than the others, that I have put my whole heart into that atrocious book, all my compassion, all my religion (travestied), all my hatred? It is true that I will write the contrary, that I will swear by all the gods that it is a work of pure art, mere monkey-play, a feat of acrobatics. And I will be lying through my teeth.
>
> And by the way! What is this "poesie fantaisiste" you talk about? I can't make head nor tail out of it. I defy Deschanel to explain what he means, just as I defy any journalist or professor to explain the meaning of a single one of the words that he uses. So now there is Fantasy Poetry, and poetry that is not Fantasy

131

Poetry! What sort of art is that which is not based on the artist's or poet's fantasy – that is to say, on his way of sensing things?

And on the subject of sentiments, heartfelt emotion, and other feminine garbage of that sort, keep in mind the profound comment of Leconte de Lisle: *All those elegiac poets are guttersnipes.*

... Except for Chateaubriand, Balzac, Stendhal, Mérimée, de Vigny, Flaubert, Banville, Gautier, Leconte de Lisle, all the modern riff-raff of today fill me with horror. Your academicians – horror. Your liberals – horror. Virtue – horror. Vice – horror. Flowing style – horror. Progress – horror. Don't ever speak to me again of those bags of wind.

These lines, or rather, these cries of fury, date from February 18, 1866. Baudelaire scribbled them at Brussels, scarcely stopping for breath, as though he had some premonition of the fact that all means of communication with the world would soon be taken from him. At the end of March he was stricken with aphasia. To heighten the terror of this dreadful misfortune, his right side was paralyzed by hemiplegia. He was able neither to speak nor to write. Only with the greatest effort did he sometimes succeed in stammering a single word, and that word an oath, *Crénom!*, which terrified the sisters at the hospital of Saint-Jean et Sainte-Elizabeth where he was awaiting the arrival of his mother who was to bring him back to Paris. After his departure from the hospital on April 19th, the nuns had the rites of exorcism performed in his room. Without a doubt, Baudelaire was truly accursed.

DEATH

At forty-six, his physical debility, his lined features, his shock of white hair, gave him the appearance of an old man. When, on August 31, 1867, death finally overtook him at the sanatorium of Chaillet, it came as a liberator. Because of the paralysis that devastated his entire nervous system it is impossible to know whether the poet had any awareness of this liberation, whether he was deprived of those last precious moments of consciousness that he speaks about in *My Heart Laid Bare:*

To give chloroform to a man condemned to death is an act of great impiety, for that would be to deprive him of the knowledge of his grandeur as a victim and to rob him of his chances of winning Paradise.

Winning Paradise.... For the last twenty years of his life his thoughts always came back to this. Surely this paradise had always dwelt somewhere within himself, but illness, worry, anguish, and the hostility of the public clouded over the vision that he had formerly glimpsed through his reveries, through his futile search for terrestial happiness: faded forever "the green paradise of a child's first loves," and the artificial paradises of alcohol, opium, and hashish.

The yearning for oblivion that we find expressed in so many of his poems and letters seems to clash violently with that deep concern over personal salvation that constantly haunts his journals, yet in reality, as far as Baudelaire was concerned, the two sentiments were opposite sides of the same coin, both of them manifesting his ardent desire to extricate himself, by no matter what means, from the insufferable misery of his existence, the desire to escape from himself. An utterly futile task for

133

a man who was constantly tearing away the veil from his illusions. In *My Heart Laid Bare* he wrote: *"Our anxiety for salvation keeps us dangling over the future,"* and shortly after having scribbled these words he completed his "Rêve d'un curieux," dedicated to Nadar:

Do you know, as I do, the savoury taste of sorrow?
Do people say of you: "Strange fellow!" as they do
                                                    [of me?
– I was at death's door. My yearning soul
Felt desire tinged with horror – a nameless malady:

Despair and ardent hope, without factious whim.
As the sands ran low in fate's hourglass
My torture grew more exquisite and grim,
My heart let the familiar world slip past.

I was like a wide-eyed child, eager for the play,
Loathing the curtain, as we loath what's in the way . . .
There came at last the truth's cold chill;

I died without surprise, and the terrible dawn
Enveloped me. – What! is that all it is?
The curtain went up and I waited still.
                         (Translated by Helen R. Lane)

Death here is nothing more than endless expectation. But this is one of the many masks She wears in Baudelaire's works. In all ages, in all languages, Death has certainly been a common enough poetical theme, but with Baudelaire it is something more (to use Gautier's phrase) than a prop used by poets, since the beginning of time, to meet their daily expenses. Except for Villon no other French poet can be said to have lived on such familiar terms with Death. Who else but Baudelaire could have said of Her that She "turns down the beds of the poor and the naked?"

134

BAUDELAIRE AND VICTOR HUGO

When Baudelaire was beginning his literary career, Hugo, not yet forty, was already a celebrity. His poems, and to an even greater extent his theatrical works, had placed him among the foremost literary figures of his time.

The first meetings between Baudelaire and Hugo – and there were to be very few of them – took place around 1842. Hugo's social charms, so it seems, had little effect on the young Baudelaire. Nor was he overawed by the prestige of the Academician whom Louis-Philippe was soon to raise to the rank of a Peer of France. Baudelaire was outspoken in his criticism of the Great Man and in his *Salon of 1845* attributes the downfall of a painter like Boulanger to the influence of Hugo and his school:

> Here is the wreckage of Romanticism, here is what comes of living in an age that accepts on faith the maxim that inspiration is everything and nothing else matters; here is the abyss to which we have been led by the rampageous and irrepressible Mazeppa. It is M. Victor Hugo who has led M. Boulanger astray, just as he has led astray so many others; it is the poet who has tumbled the painter into the ditch. M. Boulanger, let it be said, knows how to paint respectably enough (just look at his portraits) – but where the devil did he acquire his diploma as Historical Painter and Inspired Artist? Was it by studying the odes and prefaces of his illustrious friend?

In the *Salon of 1846,* new attacks against Hugo, and a bit more pointed. This time it is Baudelaire's deep admiration for Delacroix that prompts his remarks:

Eugène Delacroix has often been compared to Victor Hugo. Since we had already crowned our Romantic poet, we felt compelled to seek out a Romantic painter to share his throne. This need to find counterparts and analogies in all the different arts often leads to strange follies. . . .

M. Victor Hugo – and I have no intention of belittling his nobility and grandeur – is a craftsman who is a great deal more adroit than inventive, more correct than creative. M. Victor Hugo reveals in all his lyrical and dramatic works a perfected system of alignment and uniform contrasts. Even his eccentricities seem to adhere to certain symmetrical patterns. He has at his command, and employs with cool deliberation, all the various tones of rhythm, all the resources of antithesis, all the tricks of apposition. He is an artisan of decadence, or transition, who uses his tools with a dexterity that is worthy of both admiration and curiosity. M. Hugo was certainly an Academician before his birth, and if we were still dwelling in those bygone days of miracles and fairy-tales I would have no difficulty in believing that the green lions of the *Institut*, when they saw him pass by that wrathful sanctuary, often murmured in prophetic tones: "Thou shalt have a seat in the Academy!"

This manner of relegating Hugo to the ranks of a skillful craftsman may seem somewhat surprising, but it must be kept in mind that the Hugo of 1846 showed himself to be a very prudent administrator of his talents and a man more intent on establishing himself in his profession than in endowing French poetry with fresh tones and vigor. He no longer displayed any interest in mobilizing the youth of France for some new battle of *Hernani*. Since his reception at the Academy in 1841 he had published nothing save two small books, *Le Rhin* and *Les Burgraves*; for over a year he had occupied his place in the Chamber of Peers. Even his love affairs had taken on a bourgeois tone. In July, 1845, he had been caught *in flagrante delicto* by a jealous husband, a thoroughly banal incident that prompted Lamartine to remark: "This sort of thing is quickly forgotten, for the

French are a resilient race; no man can pass his entire life on a throne." And when this throne was a seat in the Academy or the Chamber of Peers, it is easy to see why Baudelaire refused to find in this decor the "insolence of genius" that so inspired him in the fiery personality of Delacroix. In fact, even the Hugo of the heroic days of Romanticism who had so enchanted Baudelaire the schoolboy no longer satisfied Baudelaire the artist. The dandy in him rebelled against the blatant demagogy that Hugo had allowed to creep into his work, and in the *Salon of 1846* Baudelaire has several sharp words for the *"Marion Delorme* type of literature which consists of preaching the virtue of cutthroats and prostitutes."

In a report of another art exhibition Baudelaire defends his friend Delacroix at the expense of Hugo:

I have heard so many witticisms about the ugliness of Delacroix's women, without ever grasping the humor of these remarks, that I now wish to seize this occasion to protest against such criticisms. I am given to understand that M. Victor Hugo is in on the joke. He deplored the fact – this was during the sunniest days of Romanticism – that an artist whose public renown was tantamount to his own should be so grievously mistaken in his conception of feminine beauty. He even went so far as to refer to Delacroix's women as "toads." But then, M. Victor Hugo is a great sculptural poet whose eyes are closed to spiritual things."

From 1846 to 1855 Baudelaire drifted ever farther away from Hugo. Did political opinions play a role in widening the gap between them? This is very unlikely, for politics never had much influence in determining Baudelaire's likes or dislikes. It mattered little to him that Hugo was veering rapidly toward socialism while his own inclinations were bringing him into line with the opinions of "the impeccable de Maistre." In May, 1860, he stated that if he should ever be called upon to comment on the political satires of Hugo, directed against Napoleon III, he would tend to be "more with Hugo than with the Bonaparte of the *coup d'état* of 1851," although, as he hastened to add, he considered all chatter about politics a sure sign of mental debility. Much more than their political or social differences, it was the basic opposition of their metaphysics that brought the two poets into conflict.

Nonetheless, in 1859 Baudelaire did make several advances to the exiled Hugo and dedicated a group of poems to him, *Les Petites Vieilles*, which were composed in a somewhat Hugoesque manner. The poems were sent to Hugo's "eagle nest" on the Isle of Guernsey accompanied by a letter in which, for once, Baudelaire is not parsimonious in his praise:

> The verses enclosed in this letter had been dancing about in my head for some time. The second piece was written as a deliberate imitation of your style (you may go ahead and laugh at my fatuity, I laugh at it myself) after having read several of your poems in which a truly magnificent sense of charity is blended with touchingly familiar language. I occasionally come across in the art galleries those undernourished splashers of paint who pass their time making copies of the Old Masters. Well or badly done, these imitations often contain, unknown to the painter himself, something of his own personality, something grandiose or utterly banal. This will (perhaps!) serve as an excuse for my own audacity. When the *Fleurs du Mal* reappears, swelled with three times as many new poems as the number suppressed by the law, I will have the pleasure of inscribing at the head of this section of the book the name of the poet whose works have taught me so very much and given me such great pleasure in my youth. (Letter of September 27, 1858.)

It is true that these compliments belong to the same letter in which Baudelaire requests Hugo to write a preface for his study of Gautier, but although we must not overlook the purely diplomatic aspect of this epistle, we can not doubt Baudelaire's sincerity when he congratulates Hugo for refusing the government's offer of amnesty; we know too that Baudelaire's lofty conception of his art would have made it impossible for him to subject his pen to another man's style merely to gain his good graces. While acknowledging his debt to Hugo, he does not hesitate to affirm his own originality:

> I well remember the fact that after the condemnation of my *Fleurs du Mal* you sent me a letter containing an unusual compliment, a letter in which you referred to my "withered Flowers" as a noble "decoration." At the time I did not entirely grasp your meaning, for I was overcome by anger brought on by the loss of both time and money. But today, Monsieur, I *entirely* understand what you said. I am quite content with my "disgrace" and I *know* that henceforth, no matter what form of literature I may choose to write, I shall always remain a monster and a werewolf.

At about the same time that Hugo received this letter, the first volume of his *Légende des Siècles* appeared in print and Baudelaire warmly recommended the book to his mother:

> Never has Hugo been so colorful, so startling, as in the first part of *Ratbert (Le concile d'Ancône)*, *Zim-Zizimi*, the *Mariage de Roland*, the *Rose de l'Infante*; there are flashes of blinding brilliance that only a Hugo can produce. (Letter of October, 1859.)

But with time, this enthusiasm began to wane. In February, 1860, Baudelaire wrote to the critic Armand Fraisse who had just written a eulogistic article on Hugo:

> You have not clearly distinguished between the elements of eternal beauty in Hugo's work and the laughable superstitions that he has absorbed through his concern with contemporary events; that is to say the folly, or "wisdom" of modern thought, the belief in progress, the salvation of mankind by the use of balloons, etc.

Without doubt, nothing could have irritated Baudelaire more in the Great Man's work than that certain quality that can only be referred to as demagogic. Baudelaire regarded Hugo's democratic opinions as mere crackbrained notions, but he could scarcely take them to heart since he looked on all political preoccupations as idle. He would, perhaps, have shrugged off Hugo's optimism as readily as he tolerated Malassis' universal scepticism, were it not that this optimism had the ambition (or as Baudelaire said, the folly) to sponsor a new sort of religion based on socialism and utilitarianism: the religion of Progress. But as far removed from his own ideas as those of Hugo may have been, it was not the ideas that shocked him as much as the blatantly propagandist manner in which they were expressed. All Hugo's letters from Guernsey read like manifestos. The one that he received, which was supposed to serve as a preface to his study of Gautier, appeared to Baudelaire's eyes as some sort of placard for a literary electoral campaign: "I have never said Art for Art's sake," declared Hugo, "but have always proclaimed Art for Progress' sake. In the last analysis, it is one and the same thing. . . . Forward! That is the battle-cry of Progess; it is also the battle-cry of Art. Therein lies the entire significance of Poetry. *Ite.*"

Faced with such a piece of prose as that, Baudelaire must have either burst out laughing or lost his temper. But after the age of forty, his continual poverty, his illness, and his premature debility had all but deprived him of the gift of laughter.

[handwritten note in French, partially legible:]
De Victor Hugo ... .
De Mʳ de Lamartine - auteur Religieux.
De la Religion au dix neuvième siècle -
De la Religion aimable - Mʳ Lacordaire
De M. Victor Hugo. Romantique et penseur
De Dieu au dix neuvième siècle -
De quelques idées fausses de la Renaissance Romant. que

Nonetheless, his admiration for Hugo's poetical talents permitted him to accept a commission to write another article on Hugo for an anthology that was being compiled by Jacques Crépet. It is a eulogistic piece, written while Baudelaire was still under the spell of the *Légende des Siècles,* in which he speaks with emotion of the poet's ten-year exile and nostalgically recalls the golden days of the Romantic movement when he occasionally encountered Hugo "in the company of Edouard Ourliac." The aspect of Hugo's poetry that had won his admiration as a youth, he found once again in the recent poems of *Toute la Lyre*:

> Victor Hugo was, from the very beginning, the man best equipped, best suited by nature, to express in poetry what I choose to call "the mystery of life".... The music of Hugo's verses adapt themselves to the inner harmony of nature; a sculptor, he fashions with his stanzas the unforgettable shape of things; a painter, he illuminates them in their true color. And, as though springing directly from nature, these three impressions simultaneously pierce the reader's consciousness. No other artist is so universal in scope, more adept at coming into contact with the forces of the universe, more disposed to immerse himself in nature. That which is clear and firm, he not only expresses with precision but translates in literal terms; however, he expresses with *indispensable obscurity* all that which is obscure and only vaguely perceptible.

In this study Baudelaire avoids all allusion to those aspects of Hugo's work that he utterly abhorred. When we hear him praise the charitable spirit that inspires Hugo's "tender phrases for fallen women" we can not help but wonder whether these phrases actually moved Baudelaire enough to overcome his disgust for the "Marion Delorme type of literature." And yet this is not entirely impossible, for the charms of poetry have been known to have produced even greater miracles than this. However, it is quite impossible to resist a certain feeling of uneasiness when, at the conclusion of his article, we read the affectionate terms in which Baudelaire refers to Hugo himself. The words wound us, for we know that they do not come from the heart. Although we may be willing to believe that Baudelaire, out of respect for Hugo the Poet, wishes to lay aside his ferocious disdain for Hugo the Prophet of Progress, we cannot help but deplore the fact that he speaks of him as his "beloved and venerated poet." Although it is true that Baudelaire never entirely relinquished a certain reverence for the figure of the master craftsman, he most surely did not regard him with anything resembling affection.

In April, 1862 the article that he contributed to the *Boulevard* on the first instalment of *Les Misérables*, which had just appeared, repeats and accentuates his previous praises for the compassionate spirit that impregnates "the Marion Delorme type of literature." Contrary to all his beliefs, contrary to his conviction that the idea of Progress was an absurdity (we find in *Fusées*: "Man always resembles and is always equivalent to man, that is to say, to a savage"), he presents *Les Misérables* as an edifying, and consequently "useful" work. But his true sentiments are revealed in a letter to his mother written a month later in which he states that he will probably not even spare a glance for the second instalment of the novel: "The Hugo household and its disciples fill me with horror." (Letter of May 24, 1862.)

On August 10 he is even more outspoken. He confesses to Mme Aupick that he has demonstrated, with his article on *Les Misérables*, that he "possessed the art of lying," since he had been able to write and sign his name to a eulogisitic review of *"that unclean and inept book."*

In the company of friends, he did not hesitate to pommel with sarcasms the work that he had praised in the *Boulevard*. Asselineau narrates the story and it bears the mark of authenticity, for we seem to be reading a page of Baudelaire's own prose:

"Ah!" he exclaimed in an angry voice, "where are those sentimental criminals who are full of remorse over the theft of forty sous, who debate with their consciences for hours on end, and finish by founding awards for Virtue? Do these creatures possess the same sort of reasoning apparatuses as other men? As for me, I intend to write a novel in which my hero will be a scoundrel, I mean a real scoundrel, a murderer, a thief, an incendiary and a buccaneer, and who will conclude my book with the following little speech: 'And in the soft shade of this tree planted by my own hands, surrounded by a loving family, by children that adore me, a wife that dotes on me, I savor amidst peace and tranquillity the fruits of my crimes!'"

This outburst of irony is not merely another manifestation of Baudelaire's dandyism. A dandy would have uttered those words in an icy tone, with an unruffled air. Baudelaire's "angry voice," his obvious exasperation show that he was no longer master of his temper.

The note of mockery in his *Fusées* is no less bitter. Although it is difficult to date this excerpt with any sort of precision, it seems likely that it belongs to the period of his article on *Les Misérables*:

> Hugo thinks a great deal about Prometheus. He has placed an imaginary vulture on a breast that is never lacerated by anything more than the flea-bites of his own vanity. Then the hallucination changes form, complications set in, following the logical progression described by physicians, and he begins to believe that by some *fiat* of Providence the Isle of Jersey had been metamorphosed into Saint Helena.
>
> Hugo-the-Almighty always has his head bowed in thought; no wonder he never sees anything except his own navel.

And yet, on December 17, 1862, Baudelaire again turned to Hugo for support, this time requesting him to use his influence in obtaining a Belgian publisher for his work. Only illness and anxiety can explain (not the banal expediency of this request, which scarcely needs explanation) the falsehood that Baudelaire employs in the letter when he includes Hugo among those of this friends for whom he has "the greatest affection and esteem."

Hugo, although he consented to help Baudelaire, was not taken in by him. On December 22 he wrote to Paul Meurice: "Baudelaire asked me to give him a letter of introduction to Lacroix and the Belgian group. . . . I am told that I can consider him as almost an enemy. Nonetheless, I will do him the favor that he requests."

The introduction to Lacroix was to come to nothing, but Baudelaire, his departure for Brussels temporarily postponed, could still count on Hugo's support when, in April, 1862, he took it into his head to dispatch a letter to the *Figaro* in which he denounced the manner in which the Shakespeare Commemorative Celebration was being transformed into a "Hugo Festival" by the machinations of the Great Man's followers. There is little doubt that Baudelaire was quite correct in his observations but one can not help but feel that his action was lacking in both tact and taste. Neither the fanaticism nor folly, true or supposed, of Hugo's disciples can excuse this oblique attack on a political exile. Yet the very fact that he chose the *Figaro* as his battleground demonstrates that he had fallen on very bad days indeed: how could he ever bring himself to associate his name with the very publication that had instigated, just seven years before, the prosecution of the *Fleurs du Mal*?

After this incident Baudelaire no longer refers to Hugo except in his correspondence. The gradual decline of his intellectual powers during this last painful period of his life prevented him from bringing to completion any sort of literary work. His letters to his mother and Ancelle from Brussels in 1865-1866 refer to Hugo – and even Mme Hugo and her sons – in terms that are almost pathological in their incessant abuse. A single spark of genuine humor flares up in these sickly letters when Baudelaire mentions to Ancelle Hugo's intention of moving to Belgium:

> It appears that he and the Ocean have had a spat! Either he has not the strength to put up with the Ocean, or the Ocean has grown weary of his company. And after all that trouble to erect a palace high up on a rock!

Hugo's *Chanson des Rues et des Bois,* which was published in October, 1865, seemed to Baudelaire to be a "horribly heavy" book. However, in May, 1866, he took the trouble to read carefully through the *Travailleurs de la Mer* and to scribble several notes in the page margins. The sparseness of these comments do not even supply us with a hint of what Baudelaire thought of the new novel. And at the end of the month he was to be overtaken by the stroke of hemiplegia that silenced him forever.

BAUDELAIRE AND SAINTE-BEUVE

In a very meager autobiographical note Baudelaire mentions Sainte-Beuve among his "literary acquaintances of the second period," that is to say, those men he came to know following his return from the Isle of Bourbon in February, 1842. It seems however, that he did not make Sainte-Beuve's acquaintance until 1844, perhaps after the time he sent him the following poem, in which he evokes his school days and in which we discover several lines that the poet will later employ, with far more success, in one of the most famous pieces of the *Fleurs du Mal*:

TO SAINTE-BEUVE

All beardless still, at ancient oak school-benches
Worn smoother and more lustrous than links of a chain
Burnished by men's bodies day on day,
We dragged our ennui dejectedly about with us,
Immured, stooped and squatting, in the solitary cell
Where, for ten years, the child drinks the bitter milk of
[studies.
In these memorable, distant days, that branded us
[forever,
Our teachers, forced to loose our classic iron collar,
Proved rebellious still to your rhymes;
We vanquished them by sheer indiscipline,
And the triumphant, headstrong schoolboy was allowed
To bray, like Triboulet, in Latin if he pleased.
Who of us, in those pale adolescent days
Dit not know the torpor and fatigue of cloistral ways,
– Eyes lost in leaden summer skies
Or blinding gleam of snow – spied upon the while,
Sharp ears erect, catching like a pack of hounds,
The far-off echo of a book, or rebel cries?

In summer most of all, when the lead roof-tops softened
[in the heat,

When the huge walls everywhere turned black with
[gloomy stains,
When the dog-days came, or hazy autumn
Lit the skies with its monotonous fire,
Set the shrill-voiced falcons, terror of the white pigeons,
To drowsing in their slender dungeons;
A season for day-dreaming, when the Muse hangs
[suspended,
A whole day through, from the clapper of a church-bell.
Where Melancholy, at noon, when all about is sleeping,
Stalks, chin in hand, along the corridor –
Her eyes darker, bluer, than those of that Nun

Whose obscene, pain-filled story is known to every-
[one –
Her footsteps slowed by ennuis known all too soon,
Her brow cold-beaded still from nocturnal languors;
– And then came sickly evenings, fevered nights,
When girls grow enamored of their bodies' delights,
Drawn to their mirrors – sterile dalliance –
To contemplate the mellow fruits of their nubility;
Italian evenings, of soft insouciance
Teaching the art of cheat-pleasures,
When somber Venus, from the dark balconies on high,
Pours waves of musk from her fragrant censers.

Caught within the conflict of these idle circumstances,
Ripened by your sonnets, readied by your stances,
I hunted out your book one night, and the message it
[contained,
I took away, locked in my heart, the tale of Amaury.
The mystic abyss lies just two steps from doubt,
This was no secret potion that I drank in drop by drop,
Attracted to the chasm's edge since I had reached
[fifteen,
I could already unravel René's sighs with ease;
Parched as I was with a strange thirst for the unknown,
It penetrated slowly, surely, down to my last artery.
I absorbed all of it: the rank vapors, the perfumes,
The soft whispering of memories dead and gone,
The long sinuous winding of symbolic phrases
– Tinkling rosary-beads of mystic madrigals:
A voluptuous book, if ever there was one.

Since then, when fast within a cluttered sanctuary,
Or when, beneath the suns of different latitudes,
The eternal cradling of dizzying ocean swells,
The ever-widening view of horizons without end,
Transport this heart toward the one divine dream,
Whether in the heavy leisures of an Indian-summer day,
Or in the chilling torpor of Frimaire,
Beneath the wreaths of pipe-smoke that mask the
[ceiling,
In every clime I've turned the profound, arcane pages
Of this book, beloved of numbed souls
Doomed by their destiny to suffer this very malady,
And I have now perfected, before the mirror,
The cruel art given me at birth (a demon was the bearer)
Of pain, to create a pleasure all the truer,
Of making the hurt bleed, scratching at the wounds.

Poet, is this curse or compliment?
I am, in your presence, like the lover meeting
A phantom face to face, whose arms stretch out,
[ensnaring,
Whose hand and eye possess, to suck in vital juices,
Charms unknown. All loved ones are naught
But vials of bitter hemlock – drunk with eyes tight shut –
My heart is pierced, and drawn by its own pain,
Approaches death each day, blessing the arrow.

(Translated by Helen R. Lane)

At the very outset of his literary career, Baudelaire
thus introduced himself as a disciple of Joseph Delorme
and a fervent admirer of Amaury, the hero of Sainte-
Beuve's novel *Volupté*. Indeed, between Sainte-Beuve
and Baudelaire, between the *Poésie de Joseph Delorme*
and the *Fleurs du Mal,* there exists a certain bond of literary kinship that Baudelaire perhaps acknowledged in his
frequent jocular references to "Uncle Beuve." In the
"biography" that Sainte-Beuve wrote of the fictitious
Joseph Delorme we come across several lines that would
not have been entirely out of place in a posthumous
edition of Baudelaire's works: "His soul fell into a state
of inconceivable chaos where monstrous hallucinations,
stupefying flashes of memory, criminal fantasies, gran-

diose conceptions that somehow went astray, wise pre-
cautions that ended in acts of madness, blasphemous
outbursts followed by periods of deep piety, all danced
in diabolical confusion against a background of the
blackest despair."

But although the relationship between *Joseph Delorme*
and *Fleurs du Mal* is readily perceptible (and a literary
genealogist could undoubtedly uncover a blood-link with
René as well), although both of these works reveal an
exceptional concern for an analysis of the poet's personal
sensations, the effect that each of them has on the reader
is very different indeed. Posterity has chosen to present
Baudelaire's work with its highest honors, while it has
relegated Sainte-Beuve's verses to some obscure corner
of the bibliophile's shelves.

Baudelaire was kinder to the *Poésies de Joseph Delorme*
than posterity has been. In his essay on Gautier (1859)
he mentions Sainte-Beuve as being one of the three poets
(the other two were Hugo and de Vigny) who, according
to him, were responsible for the renaissance of French
poetry during the momentous days of Romanticism. And
in his article on Dupont (1851) he was even more generous with his praise. In a somewhat circumspect, but
none the less conclusive manner, he does not hesitate to
rank Sainte-Beuve's poetry over that of Hugo:

Undoubtedly, some very ingenious men of letters,
some very erudite antiquarians, some versifiers who,
it must be admitted, managed to raise prosody almost
to the level of art, were mixed together in this [the
Romantic] movement and succeeded in extracting from
their common fund of talents some extremely startling
effects. Several of these writers even consented to
profit from the political developments of the time.
Navarin drew their attention to the Orient, and the
resulting philhellenism engendered a book as colorful
and exotic as an Indian shawl. [1] Every sort of Catholic

[1] This colorful and startling book is *Les Orientales* of Hugo
which Baudelaire compares with the *Poésies de Joseph Delorme,*
composed by Sainte-Beuve and presented to the public as the work
of a young medical student "who recently died of pulmonary
consumption complicated by an affliction of the heart."

or Oriental superstition found expression in songs that were both strange and scholarly. But surely we ought to prefer to those purely sensuous tones, designed to startle a child's troubled vision or pamper his languid ear, the plaints of that sickly and singular individual who, from the depths of a fictitious tomb, attempted to interest a turbulent society in his incurable melancholy.

If Baudelaire felt himself in any way indebted to the author of Joseph Delorme's poems, the least that can be said is that he decidedly paid back his debt, and with interest. It is to be regretted however, that he did this so often at the expense of Hugo. We cannot manage to repress the vague suspicion that "Uncle Beuve," in his private conversations with his disciple, insidiously encouraged the latter's hostility to Hugo. We know what sort of discreet and determined acts of maliciousness Sainte-Beuve was capable of propagating. We know too that the mere mention of Hugo's name caused him to spit venom. Whereas, after the *coup d'état* of December 2nd, Hugo chose to go into exile, Sainte-Beuve rallied to the Empire, which soon rewarded him with a professorship at the Collège de France (his lectures were regularly boycotted by the students) and later with a place in the Senate. His very sincere hatred for Hugo seems to have played a not unimportant role in determining his political behavior.

In his *Advice to Young Writers* Baudelaire wrote that one must be miserly with one's hate, for "hatred is a precious liqueur" made "with our blood, our health, our sleep, and two-thirds of our love." In his diatribe against Hugo and Co. it seems that he blended his own liqueur with a few drops of Saint-Beuve's distillation. And yet, as we have seen, when Baudelaire solicited a preface or letter of introduction from Hugo, the latter complied without the least sign of hesitation, whereas when he asked Sainte-Beuve, a critic by profession, for a few lines on himself or Poe . . . he received only silence.

Sainte-Beuve published nothing about Baudelaire except in the most incidental fashion: first, in February, 1860 in a brief defensive statement written in reply to a sharp and just criticism of his silence; then, in January, 1862, in an article referring to the forthcoming elections to the Academy where Baudelaire's candidacy had stirred up controversy and curiosity. 'On this occasion Sainte-Beuve finally found something to say about the *Fleurs du Mal,* the second edition of which had already appeared almost a year before. Although he had had ample time to reread and reflect upon the book, he was able to discover in it nothing more than a collection of deliberately bizarre pieces destined for the delectation of the "happy few": "This strange kiosk, carefully constructed of a composite and highly original patchwork, which for some time now has been calling attention to the furthermost Kamchatka of Romanticism, I would baptize *La Folie Baudelaire.*"

As we examine these words today, we see that they do not contain anything that could, in 1862, possibly injure their writer's reputation or compromise his academic, social, or political standing; they could not even have offended the magistrates who condemned the *Fleurs du Mal.* And as far as the general public was concerned, to relegate a French poet to the desolate wastelands of Kamchatka could scarcely be regarded as a manifestation of overwhelming approval.

All the same, this very reserved nod of recognition from the famous critic delighted Baudelaire. He had been waiting so very long for "Uncle Beuve" to recognize his existence in print that the most furtive sign of goodwill, the most discreet wink of the eye, could not fail to fill him with gratitude. This article of Saint-Beuve's which was primarily concerned with a suggested reform in the electoral procedures of the Academy, and where Baudelaire found himself mentioned only because of his status as a candidate, gave the poet more joy than a pertinent account of his work would have done, coming from another but more sincere pen. Indeed, what Sainte-Beuve had to say about his person interested him more than what he had to say about his poetry.

In fact, Sainte-Beuve had deemed it wiser to call attention to the gentlemanly appearance of Baudelaire than to certain qualities, which he certainly misunderstood, of the *Fleurs du Mal*: "There is no doubt," he wrote, "that M. Baudelaire gains by being seen in person; where one expected to see a strange and eccentric individual, one sees before one a very polite candidate, a respectful, exemplary candidate, a nice sort of fellow, refined in his speech and classical in his formality." Baudelaire could very well have taken offense at such a "testimonial," which clearly gives the impression that his work denotes the presence of a madman or demon. At another time, and from another writer, he would certainly not have swallowed such humiliating innuendos. But in January, 1860, overcome by worries, plagued by process-servers, haunting the Ministry of State in hope of some sort of financial aid, he was only too happy to be referred to as a man of the world by one of the Academicians whose support he was attempting to enlist. And thus the note of jubilation in the letter of thanks that he addressed to Sainte-Beuve:

A few words, my dear friend, to give you an idea of the very exceptional sort of pleasure that you have given me. I have been deeply wounded in recent years (though I never said anything about it) to hear myself referred to as a werewolf, a misanthrope, a sullen scowler. . . .

In short, my dear friend, you have put things straight and I am very grateful for that, I who have always said that it is not sufficient to be wise, but that above all, one must be likable.

As for what you call my Kamchatka, if I often received encouragements as vigorous as that, I believe that I would find the strength to create an immense *Siberia* – but a warm and densely populated one. When I see your activity, your vitality, I am overcome with shame; fortunately, I have in my nature certain spasms and explosions that replace, though very inadequately, the mechanism of a disciplined will-power.

. . . I want, in spite of my tonsure and white hair, to speak like a little boy. My mother, who frets a great deal, is always asking me for *news*. I have sent her your article. I know the maternal pleasure she will draw from it. Thank you – for myself and for her.

151

A few days later, on February 9, Sainte-Beuve persuaded Baudelaire to renounce his candidacy for the Academy: "Let the Academy go its own way...." The advice was sound. Baudelaire would not have received a single vote – not even Sainte-Beuve's.

PORTRAIT OF SAINTE-BEUVE,
by Heim (Louvre).

CHATEAUBRIAND AND THE GREAT
SCHOOL OF MELANCHOLY

Evoking the recent death of Delacroix, Baudelaire
wrote in 1863:

> When ... this man, unique in the history of Euro-
> pean art, passed away ... we all felt something akin
> to that depression of the soul, that sensation of in-
> creasing loneliness, with which the death of Chateau-
> briand and that of Balzac had already acquainted us,
> a sensation called forth anew just recently with the
> disappearance of Alfred de Vigny. Great national
> mourning brings a decline in general vitality, a clouding
> of the intellect, that resembles an eclipse of the sun;
> it is a fleeting likeness of the world's end.
>
> *(The Life and Work of Eugene Delacroix)*

Chateaubriand is one of that handful of writers whom
Baudelaire considers to be masters of French literature,
and indeed of world literature. He names him, together
with Victor Hugo and Balzac, as one of those who "make
the universe jealous of us." [1] He ranks him, along with
La Bruyère and Buffon, among those masters who are
"the surest and the rarest from the point of view of
language and of style." [2] He quotes passages from
Chateaubriand in his *Salon of 1859,* referring to paintings
of Delacroix in which he sees "the same breadth of touch
and feeling that characterizes the pen that wrote *The
Natchez.*" He cites other passages from Chateaubriand
in his intimate journals, in which a brief note such as
this on style, for instance: "The eternal note, the eternal,

[1] *Théophile Gautier,* a literary note (Poulet-Malassis and de
Broise, 1859).
[2] "Reflections on some of my contemporaries" (*"Réflexions sur
quelques-uns de mes contemporains"*), *Revue Fantaisiste,* July 15,
1861.

cosmopolitan style. Chateaubriand, Alph. Rabbe, Edgar Poe" – suggests the nature and the quality of the rapture that came over him at the sound of the Viscount's "organ music."

Among notes he took for an article on Laclos and the *Dangerous Liaisons* [*Les liaisons dangereuses*] is a phrase borrowed from *The Natchez*: "I was ever a man of virtue without pleasure; I would have been a criminal without remorse," a statement which Baudelaire would have promptly seconded, and one he might have chosen as the epigraph of the *Fleurs du Mal*.

To Baudelaire Chateaubriand's voice seems comparable "to the voice of great seas," [3] and in the *Artificial Paradises* he further specifies that it is the tone of this voice that enchants him, as does that of the *Suspiria de profundis* of De Quincey, of whom he says:

> In general, this is what I like to refer to as the tone of *one come back from the dead;* an accent not supernatural, but rather almost alien to humankind, half earthly, half unearthly, that we sometimes find in the *Memoirs from beyond the tomb (Mémoires d'outre-tombe)*, when anger and wounded pride have fallen silent and the scorn of the great René for the things of this earth becomes wholly selfless.

Baudelaire sees in Chateaubriand the creator of the "great school of Melancholy" (and proudly proclaims his own affiliation with that school); he considers him to be "marked by its prime talent," which is "to sing of the painful glory of melancholy and ennui." [4]

If we add that he also admires him for having been "a great aristocrat, great enough to be cynical" – that is to say a *grand seigneur* who chooses to be a snob and deliberately becomes one – it is quite apparent that Baudelaire had intended to write an impassioned defense of Chateaubriand in answer to such a man as Villemain, and had put together the basic elements of his reply:

[3] "The wit and style of Monsieur Villemain" ("*L'esprit et le style de M. Villemain*") in *Oeuvres posthumes*, Mercure de France, 1908.

[4] *Théophile Gautier*, a literary note (Poulet-Malassis and de Broise, 1859).

154

Villemain represents an officious, caviling futility akin to that of Thersite. He pads his sentences with useless details; he has no notion of the art of writing a sentence, nor likewise of the art of constructing a book.

[On Villemain's hatred of Chateaubriand:] He has the limited critical faculty of a pedagogue, and cannot appreciate the great gentleman who seeks, in a world falling to pieces, to return to life in the wilds.

In discussing Chateaubriand's early days in the regiment, Villemain censures his foppery. He censures the fact that incest was the source of his genius. I myself care nothing about the source, so long as I take pleasure in his genius!

He later blames him for the death of his sister Lucile. He constantly taxes him with a lack of sensibility. A Chateaubriand does not have the same sort of sensibility as a Villemain.

The sedentary schoolmaster [Villemain] finds it singular that the traveler [Chateaubriand] dressed in the costume of a native and a woodsman. He reproaches him for the duel for fame he fought with Napoleon. Well and good I say: wasn't this one of Balzac's passions? *Napoleon* is a name that stands for domination, and reign for reign there are some who may prefer that of Chateaubriand to that of Napoleon.

The Villemains of this world will never understand that the Chateaubriands have a right to immunities and indulgences which all the Villemains who ever live can never hope to attain.

PALESTRINA.
(en habit noir)

We do not know who this "Palestrina" is; and a notation reading "an idiot out in the rain"—added to the drawing in a hand that is not Baudelaire's—does not serve to identify him either.

BALZAC, OR THE PASSIONATE VISIONARY

Baudelaire mentions Balzac among his "first literary connections," and we know that one of his earliest published texts was an anecdotal article entitled *How a Man of Genius Pays His Debts,* in which he does not hesitate to amuse himself at the expense of the great novelist.

Balzac is here introduced sadly pacing up and down that "double arcade of the Opera" which was to vanish in 1925 with the completion of the Boulevard Haussmann:

> Yes it was unmistakably he, he, the greatest commercial and literary wizard of the nineteenth century, he, whose poetic brain was as full of figures as a banker's files; yes he, the man of mythological bankruptcies, of hyperbolic and phantasmagoric enterprises – magic lanterns which he somehow always forgot to light; the great pursuer of dreams, ceaselessly "in search of the absolute"; he, the most amazing, the most amusing, the most interesting and the most conceited of all the characters of the *Comédie Humaine*; he, that eccentric, as insupportable in real life as he is delightful in his writings, that enormous infant, stuffed with genius and vanity, who possesses so many admirable qualities, and so many defects, that one would hesitate to cut away the former for fear of losing the latter, and thus spoiling the whole fabric of this incorrigible and self-willed monstrosity!

Although the playful maliciousness of this article does not conceal its author's genuine affection for Balzac and his admiration for his talents, its general tone was such that Eugène Crépet saw fit to interpret it as a diatribe,

157

qualify the mockery as "virulent," and even deduce that Baudelaire's indignation was aroused at the sight of his eminent colleague having recourse to "ghost" writers and signing his name to shoddy texts in the interest of monetary gain.

In our opinion, far from thinking that Baudelaire intended to censure Balzac, we are inclined to believe that he was merely making sport of some of his friend's more colorful foibles by reflecting the novelist's image in a sort of trick mirror that distorted and exaggerated his already extravagant features. The very fact that this article appeared unsigned in the "humor" section of a small newspaper (*Le Corsaire-Satan,* November 24, 1845) seems to indicate that it was not intended as an attack but rather as a sort of mystification, in which neither admiration nor friendship were excluded.

Furthermore, in his other writings Baudelaire has little but praise for the man whom he refers to in his *Paradise artificiels* as "our cherished and magnificent Balzac." The only reservation he has about Balzac's work is on its style, and even on this point he grants the novelist the merit of being aware of his weakness:

> It is said that Balzac scars his manuscript and proof-sheets in an extravagant and disorderly fashion. In this way a novel undergoes a series of geneses, in which not only the unity of the sentences is disrupted, but the unity of the work itself. It is undoubtedly this strange method of creation that often gives his style that indeterminate quality of diffuseness, abruptness, and lack of polish – the sole defect of that great historian of the contemporary scene. *(Advice to Young Writers)*

> To possess not only a style, but what is more, a particular style, was one of the greatest ambitions, if not *the* greatest ambition of the author of the *Peau de Chagrin* and the *Recherche de l'Absolu.* In spite of the fact that his sentences are often heavy and entangled, he was always a connoisseur of the most subtle and the most difficult. *(Théophile Gautier)*

In the chapter of his *Salon of 1846* where he discusses

158

the beauty and heroism of modern life, Baudelaire even allows himself to get a bit carried away:

> The heros of the *Iliad* can not hold a candle to you, O Vautrin, O Rastignac, O Birotteau – and you, O Fontanarès, who dared not tell the public of the worries that you carried under that furrowed, funereal frock coat which all of us must bear – and you, O Honoré de Balzac, you, the most heroic, the most unusual, the most romantic and the most poetic of all the characters that you have torn from your breast!

In his article on Théophile Gautier he insists on Balzac's powers as a creator and on his ability to lift the "novel of manners" above the level of platitudinous observations to which it had been condemned:

> If Balzac has managed to make something admirable out of this plebeian genre, something always interesting and often sublime, it is because he has thrown his whole being into his work. I have often been dumbfounded by the remark that Balzac's chief glory lies in his powers of detached observation; it has always seemed to me that he was above all else a visionary, a passionate visionary. All his characters are endowed with the vital force that he himself possessed. All his inventions are as deeply nuanced as dreams. From the topmost pinnacles of the aristocracy to the lowest depths of the working classes, all the actors of his *Comédie* are more eager for life, more energetic and ruthless in battle, more patient in adversity, more gluttonous in joy, more angelic in devotion, than the people who act out the dramas of this real world in which we live. In short, every one of Balzac's characters, even his lackeys, has a spark of genius; every one of them is armed with a soul, loaded to the muzzle with will-power. And here we have Balzac himself. Since, to his eye, all the creatures of the exterior world appeared to stand out in high relief, somewhat larger than life, he saw fit to distort his characters, to blacken their shadows and illuminate their brighter aspects. Moreover, his insatiable appetite

for detail, which sprang from an immoderate desire to see all, to know all, obliged him to emphasize the main lines in order to conserve the overall perspective of his work. He sometimes makes me think of those engravers who, never content with their first incisions, convert into deep ravines the principal lines on their plates. We owe some marvelous things to his amazing disposition. And yet, this same disposition is often referred to as Balzac's great defect. Speaking more precisely, it is his great merit. And who else can claim to possess such prodigious talents; who else can put into operation a system that permits the writer, with a few strokes of the pen, to clothe trivialities in sunlight and splendor? Who else can do that? But to speak frankly, he who can not, can do very little indeed.

According to Baudelaire, "Balzac – enormous, terrifying, complex too – personified this monster of a civilization, with all its conflicts, all its ambitions, all its rages." [1] He even makes so bold as to qualify him as the "prodigious meteor that will cover our nation with a cloud of glory; a strange and luminous North Star, an aurora borealis flooding the frozen deserts with its magic lights." [2]

[1] *Théophile Gautier*, Poulet-Malassis et de Broise, 1859.
[2] *M. Gustave Flaubert, L'Artiste*, October 18, 1857.

MOLIÈRE AND BÉRANGER:
THE PATRON SAINTS OF PROGRESS

In Baudelaire's *My Heart Laid Bare* we come across the following note:

> The ridiculous religions of modern times.
> Molière.
> Béranger.
> Garibaldi.

At first glance, the grouping of these three men seems to present a disturbing incongruity. And yet, when Baudelaire jotted down these names in 1860 he was following what was for him a very coherent line of reasoning. Here were the three foremost saints of a new religion, a religion against which he had often vented his anger, the religion of Progress.

[handwritten manuscript facsimile]

In 1860 the liberal press, much to Baudelaire's scornful indignation, had greeted Garibaldi as a sort of new messiah, the banner-bearer of republicanism, marching

161

out to the conquest of universal happiness. As for Molière and Béranger, both men were, to Baudelaire's way of thinking, guilty of having sacrificed their art to demagogism, the former with his *Tartuffe,* the latter with his politically flavored songs. We again find these two names linked in a draft that Baudelaire wrote for a preface to the second edition of the *Fleurs du Mal:*

France is passing through a phase of vulgarity. Paris – the center and propagator of universal stupidity. In spite of Molière and Béranger, it seems incredible that France could have traveled so far down the road of *progress.*

And it appears that he also had these two authors in mind when, in another draft for the same preface, he alludes to "several celebrated hacks," who have contributed their support "to the natural stupidity of mankind."

In the case of Molière, it is clear, as Jacques Crépet and Georges Blin have already pointed out, that Baudelaire was echoing Joubert's reproachful comment that the author of *Tartuffe* had "toyed with certain superficial manifestations of religion. " In *My Heart Laid Bare* we find a similar complaint:

My opinion on *Tartuffe* is that it is not a play, but rather a pamphlet. An atheist, supposing him to be nothing more than a reasonably educated individual, would, after watching this spectacle, come to the conclusion that one must not allow certain important questions to be bandied about by the mob.

Certainly Baudelaire had not always professed such intransigent opinions on the observance of religious propriety. Certainly he was not hampered by such scruples when he published, in the *Revue de Paris* (October, 1852), "Le Reniement de Saint Pierre" which almost brought the law down on him. But neither the creator of the hearty Chrysale nor the songster of Lisette and the Roi d'Yvetot had ever won his esteem. Nothing was farther removed from his ideal of the dandy than these two writers whose vulgarity he abhorred. As early as 1848 we find him making mock of these two public idols in a sort of gossip column that he both contributed to and edited for a Paris newspaper:

> Just as the immortal Molière sometimes consulted his servant girl, so our illustrious songwriter Béranger, we are told, never scorns the advice of his housekeeper, Mlle Judith. Mlle Judith, who, we have been assured, has always enjoyed all the privileges of a mistress of the house at the home of the most popular of our popular poets, had laid claim to a title befitting her rank and has solicited the poet for the honor of bearing his name. Béranger, confident in having found his own Lisette, has given his hand to Mlle Judith who, at the moment that we write this news, has the unusual distinction of calling herself Mme Béranger." (*La Tribune nationale*, June 1, 1848.)

On the eve of the trial of the *Fleurs du Mal*, in August, 1857, Baudelaire contemplated using the popularity of Béranger's ribald songs as a defensive shield for his own poems. He wrote to his lawyer, Chaix d'Est-Ange:

> Be sure to quote (with horror and disgust) the stinking filth of Béranger: *Le Bon Dieu, Jeanneton . . .*

And in a memorandum in which he suggests several arguments to be employed in his defense, he writes:

> M. Charles Baudelaire, why should he not have the right to claim the same licenses of expression granted to Béranger (authorized complete works)? Such and such a subject that you reproach M. Ch. Baudelaire for employing has also been treated by Béranger; which one do you prefer: the sad or the gay and brazen poet, the horror in evil or the delight in it, the remorse or the impudence?

As for Chaix d'Est-Ange, he thought it wiser not to condemn the liberties in Béranger's verses; on the contrary, he deemed it more prudent to look on them as just and natural, in order to claim, if not identical, at least equal liberties for his client. For the same reason, he pleaded that the author of the *Fleurs du Mal* be granted the same freedom to portray the dreadful face of vice as Molière was allowed in *Tartuffe*. By an ironic twist of fortune, Baudelaire found himself enlisting in his defense two authors whom he never failed to abuse.

It must be said however, that Molière received a much smaller portion of this abuse than Béranger. If Baudelaire denounced Molière as a "freethinker," heir of Voltaire and the editors of the *Siècle,* he also found some praise for his "poetic good humor, so necessary for the creation of the truly grotesque" and his "solid and ungainly sense of comedy." His disdain for Béranger was total and uncompromising. One of his last texts, a draft for an open letter that he intended to address to Jules Janin in 1865, demonstrates that even at the very end of his life Béranger's name never failed to provoke his derision.

In a somewhat foolhardy article Janin had ventured to confront the melancholy temperaments of Byron and Heine with the "charming intoxication of budding youth" celebrated by the French poets, from Desportes to Béranger, whom the Empire had just honored with an eleborate official funeral.

Baudelaire hastily sketched out his indignant reaction:

I would be curious to find out whether you are entirely convinced that Béranger can be ranked as a poet. (I did not believe that people still had the nerve to speak of that man.)

And whether you are entirely convinced that fine funerals are a proof of the genius and integrity of the deceased (as for me, I believe just the contrary, that is to say, that it is usually only rogues and fools who receive fine funerals).

Béranger? There have been several true stories circulating about that coarse lout. There will be many more to be told. Let us talk of other things.

CHRONOLOGY

1821-1867

1821. April 9: Charles Pierre Baudelaire is born, at Paris, 13 rue Hautefeuille.

1827. February 10: Death of his father at the age of sixty-seven. — Changes of domicile: his mother, a widow at the age of thirty-three, moves first to 58 rue Saint-André-des-Arts, then to 30 place Saint-André-des-Arts. — During the summer months, sojourn at the the small suburban cottage, 11 rue de Débarcadère, adjacent to Ternes and Neuilly, near the Bois de Boulogne.

1828. Mme Baudelaire re-marries with Commandant Aupick, thirty-nine years of age.

1832. Baudelaire placed as a boarder at the Collège de Lyon where his parents have just set up house, his stepfather having been promoted to the rank of lieutenant-colonel and named staff-commander of the 7th military division.

1836. Return to Paris where Colonel Aupick has been transferred to the 1st military division. Baudelaire boarder at the *lycée* Louis le Grand.

1839. April: Baudelaire is expelled from Louis le Grand for lack of discipline; he completes his preparation for the *baccalauréat* at the Pension Lévêque and Bailly, rue de l'Estrapade. — August 12: he receives his degree.

1841. Independent of his family in Paris. First literary acquaintances: Édouard Ourliac, Gérard de Nerval, Balzac, Gustave Le Vavasseur. — June 9: Baudelaire embarks on a long sea voyage, following the directive issued by the Aupicks who are alarmed by his dissolute existence at Paris and by his obstinate refusal to dedicate himself to any other career save that of a writer. — September: he visits the Isle of Maurice. — October: Sojourn on the Isle of Bourbon. Then, voyage as far as India.

1842. Return to Paris. Second group of literary acquaintances: Théophile Gautier, Théodore de Banville. — June: he rents a room on the Ile Saint-Louis, 10 (today 22) Quai de Béthune. – Beginning of his liaison with Jeanne Duval, a mulatto woman who plays walk-on parts in a small theatre.

1843. He collaborates with Ernest Prarond (the same age as himself) on a play in verse, *Ideolus*, which is never to be brought to completion. – April: new domicile, rue Vaneau. – September: article refused by the *Tintamarre*, which finds its satire too audacious. – October: he returns to the Ile de Saint-Louis where he has rented, at 17 quai d'Anjou, one of the apartments in the Pimodan mansion, former residence of Lauzun. – November-December: articles refused by the *Tintamarre* and the *Démocratie pacifique*, who judge them libelous or immoral. He has now written some fifteen of the poems which will later figure in the *Fleurs du Mal*.

1844. March: publication, by Cazel, booksellers, of an anonymous work entitled *Mystères galans des théâtres de Paris*, written in part by Baudelaire. – July: Mme Aupick, seeing her son running ever deeper into debt, starts legal proceedings to have his money placed in the hands of an administrator. – September 21: the civil court sanctions his family's choice of administrator, Ancelle.

1845. April: Baudelaire's first signed work, the *Salon de 1845*, is published by Labitte: a 72-page pamphlet with yellow jacket. – May 25: appears in the *Artiste*, the sonnet "À une dame créole" which which will later be found in the *Fleurs du Mal*. – June 30: suicide attempt (with a knife) after having drawn up a will in which he bequeaths all that he owns to his mistress Mlle Jeanne Lemer (also known as Jeanne Duval). – July: stay with his mother at the official residence of the Gen. Aupick, 7 place Vendôme. Further arguments with his family and new rupture with his stepfather. Baudelaire takes a room at the Hôtel de Dunkerque, 32 rue Laffitte. – November 24: he publishes, unsigned, in the *Corsaire-Satan* a fantasy on Balzac, *Comment on paie ses dettes quand on a du génie*, which will appear several months later, this time signed, in another newspaper.

1846. January-April: contributes to the *Corsaire-Satan* and the *Esprit public*. – His address in the spring is 33 rue Coquenard (today rue Lamartine) and, a short time later, 24 rue de Provence. – May: the firm of Michel Lévy publishes his *Salon de 1846*. On the back of the volume is announced the imminent publication of a collection of poems by the same author to be entitled *Les Lesbiennes* (this book will appear eleven years later under the title of the *Fleurs du Mal*). – September 6: he publishes in the *Artiste* the poem "l'Impénitent" ("Don Juan aux Enfers"). He becomes a regular contributor of unsigned articles to the *Tintamarre* and continues to work on the staff of this review until March, 1847. December 13: in the *Artiste* his poem "À une Indienne" ("À une Malabaraise").

1847. January: the Bulletin of the Society of Men of Letters contains Baudelaire's novelette *la Fanfarlo.* — Over the course of the year his relations with his mother become more tense and embittered. He occasionally lodges at the home of Jeanne Duval, 6 rue Femme-sans-tête. Another address, 15 cité d'Orléans, is given in a passionate letter written to the actress Marie Daubrun, who conquered his affections and whom he tried to seduce. The Salon of 1847 refuses Courbet's portrait of him: *L'Homme à la pipe* (today in the Montpellier Museum). — November 14: Champfleury, in a column in the *Corsaire-Satan,* prints Baudelaire's sonnet "les Chats." — December: Baudelaire moves to 36 rue de Babylone at about the same time that General Aupick assumes command of the École Polytechnique and sets up house at 66 rue de Clichy.

1848. January: contributes regularly to the *Corsaire-Satan.* — End of February: takes part in the political riots, joins the Société Républicaine Centrale founded by Blanqui and publishes, with his friends Champfleury and Toubin, a socialist review, *le Salut public,* which expires after two issues. — April-June: staff-editor of the conservative newspaper *la Tribune nationale.* The Aupicks leave for Constantinople where the general has been assigned the post of "ministre plénipotentiare." Several days before his departure, the general reproaches Baudelaire for not breaking off relations with Jeanne Duval, who is both quarrelsome and unfaithful. Complete rupture between Baudelaire and his mother. — June 22-25: he participates in the workers' insurrection. — July 15: he publishes a translation of Poe in *la Liberté de Penser.* — October: Baudelaire goes to Châteauroux to accept the position of editor-in-chief of the bi-weekly review *le Représentant de l'Indre,* of conservative leanings. At the end of a week he is forced to relinquish the post and return to Paris. — November: the publisher Michel Lévy announces the publication, for February, 1849, of a collection of poems by Baudelaire to be entitled *Les Limbes* (this is the book that was previously announced as *Les Lesbiennes* and which will finally appear, seven years later, under the title *Fleurs du Mal*). — December: Baudelaire publishes in the *Echo des Marchands de Vins* his poem "le Vin de l'Assassin."

1849. We know very little about the life of Baudelaire for this year. He already expresses his admiration for the music of Wagner, although the first performance of *Tannhauser* is not to take place in Paris until 1850. He has the manuscript of his poems copied by a professional calligrapher and bound in grain-leather. He makes the acquaintance of Auguste Poulet-Malassis, son of an Alençon printer, who has recently been released from the galleys where he was imprisoned for his participation in the uprising of June, 1848. — December 3: Baudelaire leaves for Dijon. The reason for this journey remains a mystery although it is possible that he had received the offer of a position on some local newspaper, as was the case at Châteauroux. What is certain, however, is that he had the intention of making a long stay in that town, for he set about inquiring after a furnished apartment that he could rent for an indefinite time.

1850. January 9: Jeanne Duval joins him at Dijon. — During the poet's stay at Dijon, secondary symptoms of a syphilitic infection contracted several years before begin to manifest themselves. — The date of his return to Paris is not known. Asselineau mentions visiting him in a lodging near the boulevard Poissonnière sometime in 1850. This visit probably took place before the month of May, at which date Baudelaire is known to be residing at Neuilly, 95 avenue de la République, where he will remain until July, 1851. — June: he publishes in *le Magasin des Familles* two poems: "Châtiment de l'orgueil" and "Le Vin des honnêtes gens" (later entitled "l'Ame du Vin").

1851. March: Baudelaire gives to the *Messager de l'Assemblée* his study *Du vin et du haschich.* — April 9: under the collective title of *Les Limbes,* the *Messager de l'Assemblée* prints eleven of the poems that will later appear in the *Fleurs du Mal.* — Beginning of June: General and Mme Aupick, returned from Constantinople, take up lodgings in the Hôtel du Danube, rue Richepanse, before leaving for the French embassy at Madrid. Mme Aupick finds her son living in squalid poverty. — July: Mme Aupick departs to join her husband who has already left for Madrid. Baudelaire leaves Neuilly to live at 25 rue des Marais-du-Temple. He contributes to the *République du Peuple,* a "democratic almanac." He attempts, without success, to interest the newspaper *le Pays* in his articles on the art of caricature, which will not find· a publisher until six years later. — August: he publishes his study on Pierre Dupont. — October: he orders from London the complete works of Edgar Poe. — November 27: he publishes in the *Semaine théâtrale* an article entitled "les Drames et les Romans honnêtes." — December 2: *coup d'état.* Baudelaire will later record: "My fury at the *coup d'état.* How many musket shots I brushed off! Another Bonaparte! What shame!" But the details of his comportment on that fateful day are shrouded in mystery.

1852. January 22: the *Semaine théâtrale* prints his article on the "École païenne." — February 1: in the last issue of the *Semaine théâtrale,* forced to cease publication for lack of funds, appear two poems of Baudelaire: "les Deux Crépuscules." With Charles Monselet, Champfleury, André Thomas, and Armand Baschet, Baudelaire considers launching a new weekly-review, to be called *le Hibou philosophe,* to take the place of the defunct *Semaine théâtrale.* The project comes to naught when the "angel," on whom the would-be editors were counting, suddenly backs down. — February 23: Baudelaire offers to the *Bulletin* of the Society of Men of Letters

a short story, which the Society rejects, and which has never been recovered. — March-April: he published in the *Revue de Paris*, thanks to the influential recommendation of Gautier, the first important study on Poe to be printed in France. — April 7: he quits his lodgings in the rue des Marais-du-Temple and separates from Jeanne Duval, promising always to look after her financial needs, but vowing never to see her again. — May: he now resides at 11 boulevard Bonne-Nouvelle. — October: he now moves to 60 rue Pigalle. The ever-accumulating back-rent owed to his landlord will make it impossible for him to move from this address until 1854. He publishes in the *Revue de Paris* two poems ("Le reniement de Saint-Pierre" and "L'Homme libre et la Mer") and a translation from Poe; in the *Magasin des Familles*, another translation from Poe *(Philosophie d'Ameublement)*. — December 9: he dedicates and sends anonymously to Mme Sabatier a poem entitled "Á une femme trop gaie." This, under the title "Á celle qui est trop gaie," will be one of the six poems of the *Fleurs du Mal* condemned in court.

1853. January 10: in order to fulfill the terms of a contract, for which he has already violated his deadline, Baudelaire turns ín his translation of Poe's *Tales of the Grotesque* to the publisher Victor Lecou, and accepts the agreed remuneration. But the state of the manuscript being far from perfect, Baudelaire is seized by scruples and, although the text has already gone to print, orders suspension of the publication and agrees to take upon himself the debts incurred at the printer. — February 4: the daily newspaper *Paris* publishes one of his translations from Poe (" Tell-Tale Heart"). — March 1: another Poe translation appears in the *Artiste* ("The Raven"). His moral and physical misery has now reached such a point that Baudelaire is unable to reply to the offer of Roqueplan, director of the Opera, who asks him for a libretto, and to that of a fashionable theatre which requests a play from his pen. Jeanne Duval, suffering from illness, is also without money. — March 8: General Aupick is named senator; the Aupicks will return to Paris several weeks later and set up house at 91 rue du Cherche-Midi. — April 17: the *Monde littéraire* publishes an important essay of Baudelaire, *Morale du joujou*. — May: brief stay at Versailles and further anonymous poems sent to Mme Sabatier. — November 13 and 15: translations by Baudelaire appear in *Paris* ("The Black Cat" and "Morella" — both from Poe). — November 16: Death of Jeanne Duval's mother. In spite of his poverty, Baudelaire assumes the funeral expenses.

1854. January: he outlines the scenario of a play in five acts, *L'Ivrogne (The Drunkard)*, which is intended for the Odéon Theatre. The play is never to be brought to completion. — February: new group of anonymous poems sent to Mme Sabatier. In order to flee his creditors, Baudelaire is forced to hide away for ten or fifteen days in the Hôtel d'York, 61 rue Sainte-Anne. He tries in vain to persuade the *Moniteur* to accept several of his Poe translations. — May: more poems, still under cover of anonymity, sent to Mme Sabatier. He leaves the room on the rue Pigalle where he has been living for seventeen months and rents another in the Hôtel du Maroc, 57 rue de Seine. — July 25: the *Pays* begins publication of his translation of Poe's *Tales of the Grotesque* which, with several interruptions, will continue until April, 1855. He dreams of having his play, or rather, his idea for a play, accepted by the Gaîté theatre where Marie Daubrun is performing. The actress haunts his mind and, according to one of her biographers "undertook to console" the poet at this period. — December: weary of his constant wrangles with inpatient landlords, he announces to his mother that he intends to "soon return to the state of concubinage," either with Jeanne Duval or with "the other woman." We can not be certain of the indentity of this "otner woman": is she Marie Daubrun or the mysterious J.G.F. to whom he later dedicated *les Paradis artificiels*? It is about this time that he strikes up a friendship with Barbey d'Aurevilly.

1855. March-April: he changes hotels six times within a month. General Aupick purchases a small seaside house at Honfleur. — May 26: tne *Pays* begins publication of an essay by Baudelaire on the World Exhibition that was inaugurated several days before at the Nouveau Palais des Beaux-Arts, avenue Montaigne. It prints the second part in its issue of June 3rd, but refuses the last installment (on Ingres), that the *Portefeuille* agrees to accept for its August 12 edition. — June 1: the *Revue des Deux-Mondes,* using the previously unpublished title of *Fleurs du Mal,* prints a collection of eighteen poems by Baudelaire. The poet is now living at the Hôtel de Normandie, 13 rue Neuve-des-Bons-Enfants. — July 8: the *Portefeuille* publishes his essay *De l'essence du Rire.* — From July to December, Baudelaire lodges in a furnished room, 27 rue de Seine. — August 3: he discusses with the publisher Michel Lévy a possible two-volume edition of his translations of Poe, to include *Tales* and *New Tales of the Grotesque.* — November 4: the *Figaro,* commenting on the poems of the *Fleurs du Mal* published in the *Revue des Deux-Mondes,* assures its reader that "the reputation and talent" of their author "are smashed into a thousand pieces," and that Baudelaire "having lost his shock-appeal, will no longer be referred to except among the dehydrated fruits of contemporary poetry." — December: Baudelaire publishes in the *Nouvelle Galerie des Artistes dramatiques* a eulogistic notice on the actor Rouvière. — Late December: he moves to 18 rue d'Angoulême-du-Temple, this time an unfurnished room, that he does his best to make livable.

1856. March: publication date of the *Tales of the Grotesque* of

Poe, in the Collection Michel Lévy, price, one franc. —
May: Baudelaire quits the rue d'Angoulême to return to
hotel lodgings. He chooses the Hôtel Voltaire, 19 quai Voltaire, where he will remain for two years. — August or early
September: new quarrel with Jeanne Duval and another
separation. — October 21: Michel Lévy agrees to publish his
translation of Poe's *Adventures of Arthur Pym.* — December
30: Poulet-Malassis accepts for publication the *Fleurs du
Mal.*

1857 Early February: Poulet-Malassis receives the manuscript of
the *Fleurs du Mal.* — February 25: the *Moniteur* begins
publication of the *Adventures of Arthur Gordon Pym.* —
March: publication of the *New Tales of the Grotesque* by
Michel Lévy. — April 20: the *Revue Française* prints several
of the poems that are to later appear in the *Fleurs du Mal.*
— April 28: death of General Aupick at his home, 91 rue
du Cherche-Midi; Baudelaire's name appears neither in his
will nor among the funeral announcements. — May 10: the
Artiste prints several poems of the *Fleurs du Mal,* whose
publication date is imminent. — Late May: Mme Aupick
retires to Honfleur. — June 16: the Minister of Public
Education grants Baudelaire's request for a "compensation"
of 200 francs for his translation of the *Tales of the Grotesque.* — June 25: publication date of the *Fleurs du Mal,*
at the price of 3 francs: the book has been printed in an
edition of 1,300 copies. — July 5: the *Figaro* rages against
the book and its author, and after having enumerated its
choice of "guilty" poems, concludes: "Nothing can justify
a man of over thirty for putting before the public such
monstrosities." — July 16: the public prosecutor has the
edition seized and issues suit against Baudelaire and his
publisher. — August 18: for the first time Baudelaire writes
to Mme Sabatier without disguising his signature nor concealing his identity: "All these verses included between
pages 85 and 105 [of the seized book] are for you." — August
20: the court condemns Baudelaire to a 300-franc fine and
his publishers, Poulet-Malassis and de Broise to a fine of
100 francs each; it orders the removal of six poems from
the *Fleurs du Mal.* — August 24: the *Présent* publishes six
"prose-poems" of Baudelaire under the title *Poèmes noc-
turnes.* — August 31: on the day following Mme Sabatier's
complete acquiescence to his advances, Baudelaire, in a
letter in which he mixes the familiar "tu" form of address
with the more formal "vous," backs out of this liaison that
he had so ardently desired. Henceforth, his relations with
Mme Sabatier will remain rigidly "platonic." — October
1-15: the *Présent* accepts Baudelaire's essays on several
French and foreign caricaturists. — October 18: his essay on
Flaubert appears in the *Artiste.* — November 6: Baudelaire
writes to the Empress to request a cancellation of the fine
levied on his book. — November 15: the *Présent* prints
several new poems of his that will later appear in the second
and third editions of the *Fleurs du Mal.* — December 31:

Baudelaire writes to the Minister of Public Education in the hope of obtaining further financial assistance.

1858. January: Pains in the legs, difficulty in walking, shortness of breath, cramps in the stomach: ether, opium. Baudelaire contemplates joining his mother at Honfleurs; she entreats him to settle there. — January 18: the Minister of Public Education awards him a second grant of 100 francs for his translation of the *Tales of the Grotesque.* — January 20: the Keeper of the Seals reduces the fine incurred by the condemnation of the *Fleurs du Mal* to 50 francs. — Late February: Baudelaire hurls abuse at his legal guardian, Ancelle, an old friend of Mme Aupick, whose indiscreet meddling in the poet's personal affairs has greatly humiliated Baudelaire. He speaks of publicly insulting Ancelle. — March 3: Mme Aupick, terrified, sends one of her friends, M. Jacquotot, to reason with the poet, and succeeds in calming his anger. — From March 20 to April 4 or 5: stay at Corbeil where Baudelaire corrects proofs for his third volume of Poe translations, which Michel Lévy is having printed in that town. — Late April: publication of the *Adventures of Arthur Gordon Pym.* — September 19: the *Artiste* prints the sonnet "Duellum." — September 30: Baudelaire's essay on hashish appears in the *Revue Contemporaine.* — October 21; short visit to his mother at Honfleur. — Late October: he leaves the Hôtel Voltaire with the intention of settling in Hounfleur. — November: although possessing no Paris address of his own, it appears that Baudelaire is now living at 22 rue Beautreillis in Jeanne Duval's flat; in spite of their continual rows, and frequent adieus, the two of them will never break off relations. — December: he spends twelve days at Alençon where he is the guest of Poulet-Malassis. — December 31: he returns for a forty-eight-hour stay at Alençon. A genuine friendship has grown up between publisher and author, and the two men, so closely linked together in business, will never neglect each other in the difficult days ahead.

1859. January 9: Baudelaire publishes in the *Artiste* an appreciation of a volume of short stories of Charles Asselineau (*La double Vie*). January 20: two poems of his in the *Revue Française* ("Le Possédé" and "le Goût du néant"). — In the second half of January he makes another trip to Honfleur. The Minister of Public Education allots him another grant of 300 francs for his translation of the *New Tales of the Grotesque.* — February 23: from Honfleur, he sends to Maxime Du Camp the Poem *Le Voyage*, accompanied by a dedication. — Early March: he returns to Paris and resides at Jeanne Duval's. — March 10 and 20: in the *Revue Française*, two translations from Poe ("Eleonora" and "Un-événement à Jérusalem"). — March 13: The *Artiste* publishes his study on Théophile Gautier. — March 15: his poem, "Danse macabre," appears in the *Revue Contemporaine.* — April 5: Jeanne Duval, stricken with paralysis, is transported to the Dubois Sanatorium, 200 faubourg Saint-Denis, where

DRAWING BY BAUDELAIRE
According to Jacques Crépet, this may be a bit-player at the Théâtre de la Porte Saint-Martin, whom Baudelaire may have seen in the wings as he waited for Marie Daubrun.

she shall remain until May 19. – April 10: Baudelaire publishes three poems ("Sisina," "le Voyage," "l'Albatros") in the *Revue Française*. – He returns to Honfleur. – April 20: translation from Poe in the *Revue Française*. – May 20: in the same review, the poem "la Chevelure." From June 10 to July 20: in the same review, "Lettre sur le Salon de 1859." – Second half of June: Baudelaire returns to Paris. – From the beginning of August, and perhaps before that date, he has rented a room in the Hôtel Dieppe, 22 rue d'Amsterdam, but he spends most of his nights with Jeanne Duval, rue Beautreillis. – September 15: he publishes in the *Revue Contemporaine* two poems under the title of *Fantômes parisiens* ("Les sept Vieillards" and "les Petites Vieilles"). – October: the *Revue internationale*, appearing monthly in Geneva, begins publication of his translation of Poe's *Eureka*; this work is continued in the issues for November and December, 1859, and January, 1860, and is then discontinued. – November: his essay on Gautier is published in brochure form, preceded by a letter from Victor Hugo (Poulet-Malassis and de Boise, publishers; price one franc).

— November 30: three poems in the *Revue Contemporaine* ("Le Masque," "Chant d'automne," and "Sonnet d'automne"). — Early December: in spite of his own poverty, Baudelaire purchases several drawings from Guys. — December 17: short visit to his mother at Honfleur.

1860. January 1: Baudelaire and Poulet-Malassis sign a contract for the publication of four books (the second edition of the *Fleurs du Mal*, *les Paradis artificiels*, *Curiosités esthétiques*, and a collection of literary essays); each of these volumes is to be printed in an edition of 1,500 copies; the author is to be paid 300 francs per volume, one-half the sum on receipt of the manuscript, the other half on submission of the final corrected proof sheets. — January 13: minor but portentous cerebral stroke: the poet does not lose consciousness. — January 15 and 31: the *Revue Contemporaine* prints his essay *Un mangeur d'opium*. — January 22: three poems in La Causerie ("À une Madone," "le Cygne," "le Squelette laboureur"). — Late January and early February: Baudelaire deeply moved and impressed by the Wagner concert performed at the Salle des Italiens. — February 7: new government grant of 300 francs awarded him for his art criticism. — February 17: translation from Poe ("The Angel of the Odd") in *La Presse*. — May: publication of the *Paradis artificiels* in an edition of 1,200 copies instead of the 1,500 stipulated in the contract of January 1. — May 15: the *Revue Contemporaine* prints five poems ("Rêve parisien," "l'Amour du mensonge," "le Rêve d'un curieux," "Semper eadem" and "Obsession"). — July: Baudelaire rents a small apartment in Neuilly, 4 rue Louis-Philippe, and moves in with his "debris" (the odd pieces of furniture that have survived the onslaught of his creditors). He plans to divide his time between this new abode and his mother's home at Honfleur. In fact, he will remain at the Hôtel Dieppe until December, while Jeanne Duval, suffering from hemiplegia, will take over the Neuille apartment in August or early September. — October 15: eight of his poems appear in the *Artiste* ("Alchimie de la douleur," "Horreur sympathique," "l'Horloge," "les Aveugles," "À une passante," "Un fantôme," "Chanson d'après-midi," and "Hymne à la Beauté). — From October 15 to 20: stay at Honfleur. — November 15: the Minister of Public Education awards Baudelaire a 200-franc grant for "encouragement of letters." — December 15: Baudelaire moves into his Neuilly apartment, sharing it with Jeanne Duval.

1861. January 10: at the end of twenty-five days Baudelaire flees Neuilly, utterly exasperated by the continual presence of Jeanne's brother, who seems to have moved in with the couple and lives at their expense. He returns to the Hôtel Dieppe, rue Amsterdam. — Early February: publication of the second edition of the *Fleurs du Mal* with thirty-five new poems; an edition of 1,500 copies, at three francs a copy. February 28: the *Revue Contemporaine publishes* two poems ("La Voix" and "le Calumet de la Paix"). — March: Jeanne

Duval spends time in a sanitorium, while her brother sells a portion of the Neuilly furnishings. — April 1: the *Revue Européenne* prints an essay by Baudelaire on Richard Wagner. Dentu, publisher of the review, issues this essay in a brochure entitled *Richard Wagner et Tannhauser*. — April 3: the Ministry of State gives Baudelaire a grant of 300 francs. — April-May: Baudelaire notices new syphilitic symptoms: papule, rheumatism in the joints. His financial situation seems to have reached a new low; his literary career seems to be stagnant; once again his thoughts turn to suicide. — May 15: the *Revue Fantaisiste* publishes the poem *Madrigal triste*. — June 15: *Revue Fantaisiste* begins publication of a series of critical studies, under the general title *Réflexions sur quelques-un de mes contemporains*, which Baudelaire hopes to later group together in book form; the first essay is devoted to Victor Hugo. — July: Baudelaire contemplates submitting his candidature for the French Academy. — July 1: article on Marceline Desbordes-Valmore in the *Revue Fantaisiste*; on July 15: articles on Auguste Barbier, Théophile Gautier, Petrus Borel; on August 1: articles on Gustave Le Vavasseur and Théodore de Banville; on August 15: articles on Pierre Dupont and Leconte de Lisle. — September 15: four poems ("La Prière d'un Païen," "Le Rebelle," "l'Avertisseur," "Épigraphe pour un livre condamné") appear in the *Revue Européenne*; in the *Revue Fantaisiste*, article on Delacroix's mural paintings in the church of Saint-Sulpice. — October 15 in the *Revue Fantaisiste*, critical study on Léon Cladel's *Martyrs ridicules* which will, in 1862, serve as preface to the book. — November 1: the sonnet *Recueillement* appears in the *Revue Européenne*; in the *Revue Fantaisiste*, nine prose-poems. — December 11: Baudelaire informs the French Academy of his desire to be inscribed among the candidates for one of two available seats (left vacant by the deaths of Scribe and Lacordaire). He soon begins the usual round of visits required of a candidate, and before the end of the year has called on Vigny, Lamartine, Viennet, Villemain, and Patin.

1862. January 12: in the *Boulevard*, several sonnets by Baudelaire including the previously unpublished "le Coucher du Soleil romantique" and "le Couvercle." — Late January: unsigned article by Baudelaire in the *Revue Anecdotique* ("Une réforme à l'Académie"). — During the month of January Baudelaire discovers a "monstrous fact" that causes him "great unhappiness." He refuses to say anything more on this matter, but the noted Baudelaire scholar, Jacques Crépet, has put forth a theory that may very well be the key to this mystery: could it be that the so-called "brother" who was at this time living with Jeanne Duval was in reality her lover? — February 10: on the advice of Sainte-Beuve Baudelaire withdraws his candidacy for the French Academy. — March 1: several poems by Baudelaire in the *Artiste*, including the previously unpublished sonnets "le Gouffre" and "la Lune offensée." — Late March: he submits to the

Revue Anecdotique an unsigned obituary notice on his friend the novelist Paul de Molènes, one of whose short stories *(les Souffrances d'un houzard)* he had long contemplated adapting for the stage. – April 2: unsigned article in the *Revue Anecdotique* ("L'Eau-forte est à la mode"). – The Ministry of State awards him a grant of 300 francs. – April 14: Claude-Alphonse Baudelaire, a retired magistrate and half-brother of the poet, dies from the effects of a cerebral hemmorhage accompanied by a stroke of hemiplegia, at the age of 57. The poet had not seen him for about 20 years. – April 20: article by Baudelaire on *les Misérables* in the *Boulevard*. – July 12, 19, 26, and August 2: *le Monde* publishes a long translation from Poe *(Joueur d'échecs de Maelzel)*. – August 26, 27, and September 24: *la Presse* publishes twenty prose-poems (fourteen of them previously unpublished). – September 14: article in the *Boulevard* on modern painters and etchers; Baudelaire praises the work of Manet, Jongkind, Méryon, and Whistler – November 12: Poulet-Malassis is arrested on the complaints of an unpaid printer and incarcerated in the Clichy debtors' prison. – December: Malassis is transfered to the jail of the Madelonnettes, 12 rue des Fontaines-du-Temple. Baudelaire entertains the hope of becoming director of a subsidized theatre: perhaps that of the Odéon. – December 28: the *Boulevard* prints his poem "les Plaintes d'un Icare."

1863. January 13: Baudelaire yields to the publisher Hetzel the exclusive rights, for a period of five years, to a third and enlarged edition of the *Fleurs du Mal* and a volume of prose-poems *(Le Spleen de Paris)*. The contract calls for a first printing of 2,000 copies per title, and the author is to receive, for each work, the sum of 600 francs. Baudelaire immediately pockets the money, but Hetzel is never to receive the promised manuscripts. – January 25: the *Boulevard* prints a previously unpublished poem, *l'Imprévu*. – February 1: another poem in the *Boulevard*, *l'Examen de minuit*. Poulet-Malassis' bankruptcy necessitates a sale of all the works of Baudelaire in the publisher's catalogue: the second edition of the *Fleurs du Mal* and *les Paradis artificiels* are remaindered at one franc a copy, and the pamphlet on Gautier at 50 centimes. – April 22: after five months in prison awaiting trial, Malassis is condemned by the Court (the judicial records for 1863 having been burned during the Paris Commune of 1871, we do not know the details of his condemnation, except that it included a prison term.) – May 13: Baudelaire takes a lively interest in the theatrical début of a young blond actress, Mme Louise Deschamps, who plays the rôle of Andromache at the Odéon theatre; this interest is not returned. – June 10: in the *Revue Nationale et Étrangère*, two prose-poems ("Les Tentations" and "la Belle Dorothée"). – June 14: in the *Boulevard*, two other prose-poems ("les Bienfaits de la Lune" and "Laquelle est la vraie?"). – July 12: Malassis, having failed in his efforts to appeal his sentence and having seen his request for pardon rejected, is ordered to present himself to the prison authorities. — August: Baudelaire makes plans for a trip to Belgium in order to give a series of paid lectures, lend his aid to the review *l'Indépendance belge*, interest the Belgian publishers Lacroix and Verboeckhoven in some of his work, and finally, to complete several projects that he has on hand, including a new edition of his *Paradis artificiels*. — September 2 and 14 and November 22: he publishes in the *Opinion nationale* an important study on the life and works of Eugène Delacroix. — September 10: Mme Aupick spends several days in Paris. — Mid-September: Malassis flees to Belgium to escape serving his prison term. — October 10: in the *Revue Nationale*, new prose-poems ("Une mort héroïque" and "le Désir de peindre"). — November 1: Baudelaire cedes to the publisher Michel Lévy for the laughable sum of 2,000 francs the entirety of his Poe translations (the three volumes already published and two others which are shortly to appear). — Late November: publication of one of the new Poe volumes, *Eureka*. — November 26, 28, and December 3: he publishes in the *Figaro* his study on Constantin Guys: *le peintre et la Vie moderne*. This long essay is preceeded by an introductory note signed G.B., the initials of Gustave Bourdin, who, in 1857, had the distinction of instigating the legal proceedings against the author of the *Fleurs du Mal*. — December 10: new prose-poems in the *Revue Nationale* ("Le Thyrse," "les Fenêtres," "Déjà").

1864. February 7 and 14: the Figaro begins publication of the *Spleen de Paris* (prose-poems). After having printed six of the poems and announcing that the series was "to be continued," the newspaper suspends publication of this work. The editor informs Baudelaire that his prose-poems "are a bore to everyone." — March 1: the *Revue Nouvelle* prints four poems, three of which have previously been unpublished ("Sur le Tasse en Prison," "Bien loin d'ici," "les Yeux de Berthe"). — Second half of March: Fantin-Latour displays at the Salon his painting *Homage to Delacroix* in which Baudelaire figures in the foreground as one of the models. — April 14: the *Figaro* publishes an unsigned letter from Baudelaire in which he denounces the fashion in which the tercentenary celebration of Shakespeare's birth is being converted into a publicity campaign for Hugo. — April 24: Baudelaire leaves for Brussels where he takes a room in the hôtel du Grand Miroir, rue de Montagne. — From the 2nd to the 23rd of May he gives a series of five lectures at the Cercle Artistique et Littéraire (one on Delacroix, one on Gautier and three on drugs and stimulants.) He is paid only for the first two (50 Belgian francs per lecture). Except for the initial one (on Delacroix), these lectures, which were actually readings, could be termed total failures. — Baudelaire considers returning to Paris around June 15, after he has tried his luck with the publishers Lacroix and Verboeckhoven. — Late May: brief trip to Namur in order to see Rops. — June: he contem-

𝒜 Poulet-Malassis

Imp. Lemercier et Cⁱᵉ Paris.

plates writing a series of articles on Belgium for the *Figaro*, in which he will give vent to his hatred of the country and its citizens. — June 13: M. Prosper Crabbe, a Brussels stockbroker, organizes at his home a literary soirée with Baudelaire as speaker. Some thirty invitations manage to attract no more than ten guests who present a "melancholy" sight in the three spacious rooms especially decorated for the gathering. A dismal failure. — Baudelaire suffers from growing anger and exasperation, which aggravates his continual cardiac and digestive troubles. — June 23: Lacroix and Verboeckhoven are totally uninterested in publishing the works he has offered them. — August: he employs a Paris literary agent to negotiate for the sale of his *Paradis artificiels*, a collection of literary criticism and a work entitled *Pauvre Belgique!* — August 13: the *Vie Parisienne* prints one of his prose-poems ("les Projets"). — October: the poet suffers from fever every night now; although he detests Belgium, he remains at Brussels for fear, so it seems, of confronting his French creditors. — November 1: three prose-poems in the *Artiste*, only one of which is being printed for the first time ("La Fausse Monnaie"). — Early December: stay at Namur as a guest of Rops. — December 25: the *Revue de Paris* prints six prose-poems, three of which were previously unpublished ("Les Yeux des pauvres," "le Port," "le Miroir").

1865. January: the only person whose company he can tolerate at Brussels is, he says, Poulet-Malassis, who, unfortunately, lives outside the town (at Ixelles). He is however, a frequent guest of Mme Hugo, who is not indifferent to his praises of Sainte-Beuve, her former "admirer." — January 7, 14, 21, and 28: the *Monde illustré* publishes his translation from Poe, "The System of Doctor Tarr and Professor Fether" (but it is Michel Lévy, holder of the publication rights, who receives the money for the piece). — Mid-March: Michel Lévy puts on sale the fifth volume of the Poe translations: *Histoires grotesques et sérieuses.* — April 29: the *Petite Revue*, in an unsigned article by Poulet-Malassis, quotes several occasional verses written by Baudelaire in Belgium. — May 13: again through the intervention of Malassis, the same review publishes Baudelaire's sonnet "Sur les débuts d'Amina Boschetti." — June 21: the Brussels daily paper *l'Indépendance belge* prints a prose-poem ("les Bons chiens"). — June 24: Poe translation in the *Vie parisienne.* — From July 4 to 15: journey to Paris, Honfleur, and return to Brussels. The purpose of Baudelaire's rapid French trip is to collect funds to cover a bill of credit that he had given to Poulet-Malassis and that the latter now is obliged to sell — which will mean a loss of a third of the profits he was hoping to obtain from his work in Malassis' hands. Mme Aupick lends her son 2,000 francs which will permit him to partially reimburse Malassis — to whom he owes 5,000 — and to save his works from the fate he feared. — July 8: the *Petite Revue* publishes the poem "le

181

Jet d'eau." — October: Baudelaire complains of his "soporific" state which causes him to doubt his lucidity. In fact, he seems to have lost a good deal of his mental energy. Since his arrival in Belgium he has been able to finish none of the books he had outlined (a collection of critical essays and a volume of prose-poems), nor put into shape his *Pauvre Belgique!* whose title even remains uncertain (in

DELACROIX: SELF-PORTRAIT *(Louvre)*.

August he refers to it as *Une capitale ridicule,* and in December as *la Belgique déshabillée*). — October 28: he contributes an obituary notice on the actor Rouvière to the *Petite Revue.* — December: violent attacks of neuralgia; opium, digitalin, belladonna, quinine.

1866. January: dizzy spells, neuralgia, nausea. Since his Paris literary agent has had no success in placing any of his works, Baudelaire asks his legal guardian, Ancelle, to try to interest a number of publishers: Garnier frères, Dentu, etc. — March 5: a group of young poets whom he has never met and who have yet to publish a single book, salute him as their master, although his own contemporaries seem scarcely to acknowledge his existence. An unwilling exile in Brussels, Baudelaire reads in the weekly review *l'Art* a eulogy of his poems written by a certain Stéphane Mallarmé (twenty-three years old) and an enthusiastic essay devoted to him by the twenty-one-year-old Paul Verlaine. Baudelaire, who is now ill, writes to Troubet, Sainte-Beuve's secretary who had called his attention to the praises of these young unknowns: "These young people frighten the life out of me. There is nothing I want more than to be left alone." — In March, during a trip to Namur, Baudelaire is overcome by dizziness while visiting the church of Saint-Loup with Rops and Poulet-Malassis. The next day, cerebral stroke. His friends take him back to Brussels; his right side is paralyzed, his speech is halting and confused. — March 29 and 30: he is still able to dictate several

Charles Baudelaire.

22 rue d'Amsterdam.

Écrivez moi un mot pour me dire si vous croyez convenable que je demande à la Revue Nouvelle le prix de mes vers, et combien, en ce cas, il faut demander

Présentez mes respectueux amitiés à Madame Leconte de Lisle

short letters. — March 31: under the title (chosen by Catulle Mendès) of *Nouvelles Fleurs du Mal,* the *Parnasse contemporain* prints a group of sixteen of his poems, posterior to the second edition of the *Fleurs du Mal* or not included in the latter book. — From April 3 to 19: the aphasia grows steadily worse. Baudelaire, who can no longer utter more

183

than the single word "Crénom," is hospitalized in a Brussels sanatorium under the direction of nuns, the Institut Saint-Jean at Sainte-Elisabeth, rue des Cendres. Ancelle arrives in Brussels and is soon follewed by Mme Aupick, seventy-two years old, accompanied by her servant. – Late April, May-June: Baudelaire, who has been brought back to his hotel room at the Grand Miroir, receives frequent visits from his friends Stevens and Poulet-Malassis. With these friends, and his·mother, the poet, totally mute and half paralyzed, is occasionally taken for drives around the city. In April, Poulet-Malassis publishes 260 copies of a volume entitled *Épaves,* a booklet for which Baudelaire had corrected the proofs and which contains twenty-three poems, including the six condemned by the French law-court; a frontispiece by Rops adorned this edition which Baudelaire greeted "with child-like joy." – June 1: under the title *Petits poèmes lycanthropes,* the *Revue du XIXe Siècle* prints two prose-poems. – July 2: Baudelaire leaves Brussels to return to Paris in the company of his mother, her servant, and Arthur Stevens. – July 4: after spending two days in a hotel, Baudelaire is transferred to the hydrotherapeutic clinic of Dr. Émile Dumas, rue du Dôme, in the neighborhood of Chaillot. – On a petition initiated by Asselineau and signed by Banville, Champfleury, Leconte de Lisle, Mérimée, Sainte-Beuve, and Sandeau, the Ministry of Public Education agrees to pay a portion of the expenses incurred by Baudelaire at the clinic. To distract the invalid, Mme Paul Meurice and Mme Édouard Manet come by his room to play excerpts from Tannhaüser at the piano. –October 27: the *Petite Revue* publishes the prose-poem "Les Bons Chiens."

1867. August 31: Baudelaire dies at 11 A.M.

September 2: after the religious ceremonies at the church of Saint-Honoré, place de l'Hippodrome, Baudelaire is interred in the cemetery of Montparnasse. His friends Banville and Asselineau make speeches at his grave. – From August 31 to October 11, the *Revue Nationale* prints six prose-poems, of which three were previously unpublished. – November 22: Baudelaire having died intestate, and an heir on his father's side of the family having appeared on the scene, his remaining property, that is to say, his rights to his complete works, are offered at public auction. Put on the auction-block at a base price of 1,000 francs, they are acquired by Michel Lévy, already the owner of his Poe translations, on a bid of 1,750 francs.

1868. May 6: criminal court of Lille condemns, in absence, Poulet-Malassis to one year in prison and a five-hundred-franc fine for his publication of *Épaves,* and orders the destruction of all the copies of this book seized in France since is appearance two years before.

M

Vous êtes prié d'assister aux Convoi, Service et Enterrement
de Monsieur Charles Pierre **Baudelaire**, décédé à Paris
le 31 Août 1867, à l'âge de quarante-six ans, muni des Sacrements
de l'Eglise;

Qui se feront le Lundi 2 Septembre prochain, à l'Eglise
St. Honoré, sa paroisse, Place de l'Hippodrome, à 11 heures
précises.

On se réunira à l'Eglise.

De Profundis !

De la part de Madame Vve. Aupick, sa mère, de Mr.
Perée, sa grand'tante et de ses enfants, de Mme. Vve. Baudelaire,
sa belle-sœur, de Mr. Jean Levaillant, Général de Brigade, de
Mr. Jean Jacques Levaillant, Chef de Bataillon, de Mr. Charles
Levaillant, Général de Division, ses cousins.

1870. Nadar, an old friend of Baudelaire, catches sight of
Jeanne Duval in the street, hobbling along on crutches.
This is the last picture we have of her. The end of her
story is entirely unknown to history.

1871. Mme Aupick dies at Honfleur in the course of a stroke
of apoplexy.

185

LES

FLEURS DU MAL

PAR

CHARLES BAUDELAIRE

> On dit qu il faut couler les execrables choses
> Dans le puits de l'oubli et au sepulchre encloses,
> Et que par les escrits le mal resuscité
> Infectera les mœurs de la postérité ;
> Mais le vice n'a point pour mère la science,
> Et la vertu n'est pas fille de l'ignorance.
>
> (THÉODORE AGRIPPA D'AUBIGNÉ, *Les Tragiques*, liv. II

PARIS

POULET-MALASSIS ET DE BROISE

LIBRAIRES-ÉDITEURS

4, rue de Buci.

—

1857

BAUDELAIRE: A SELECTED BIBLIOGRAPHY

CRITICAL EDITIONS AND TEXTS IN FRENCH:

Baudelaire, Charles. *Les fleurs du mal*. Texte de la 2. éd., suivi des pièces supprimées en 1857 et des additions de 1868. Ed. critique établie par Jacques Crépet et Georges Blin. Paris, J. Corti, 1942.
————. *Oeuvres*. Texte établi et annoté par Y.-G. Le Dantec. Paris, Gallimard, 1932-1935. 2 vols. (Bibliothèque de la Pléiade. 1, 7.)
————. *Oeuvres complètes*. Variantes, notes et commentaires de J. Crépet et Claude Pichois. Paris, Conard, 1947-1953.
————. *Pauvre Belgique*. Texte publié par Jacques Crépet et Claude Pichois. Paris, Conard, 1953. (Unpublished manuscripts in the Collection de Spoelberch de Louvenjoul of the Institut de France.)

TRANSLATIONS IN ENGLISH:

Baudelaire on Poe, critical papers. Translated and edited by Lois and Francis E. Hyslop, Jr. State College (Pa.), Bald Eagle Press, 1952.

Baudelaire, prose and poetry. Translated by Arthur Symons. New York, A. and C. Boni, 1926. (English versions of *Poèmes en prose, Les fleurs du mal, Les Paradis artificiels*. Original Casanova Society edition, London, 1925.)

Baudelaire, a self-portrait. Selected letters, translated and edited by Lois Boe Hyslop and Francis E. Hyslop, Jr. London, New York, Oxford University Press, 1957.

Eugene Delacroix, his life and work. New York, Lear, 1947.

Poems. A translation of *Les fleurs du mal* by Roy Campbell. New York, Pantheon, 1952.

Les fleurs du mal. Rendered into English by Alan Conder. London, Cassell, 1952.

Flowers of Evil. From the French of Charles Baudelaire, by George Dillon [&] Edna St. Vincent Millay. With the original texts and with a preface by Miss Millay. New York, London, Harper, 1936.

Flowers of Evil (Fleurs du Mal). In pattern and prose by Beresford Egan and C. Bower Alcock. New York, privately printed for W. Godwin, 1933.

Flowers of Evil. Translated into English verse by various hands. Edited, with an introduction and notes, by James Laver and illustrated by Jacob Epstein. London, Limited Editions Club, at the Fanfare Press, 1940.

Flowers of Evil. Translated by Jacques Leclercq. Mount Vernon (N. Y.), Peter Pauper Press, 1958.

One hundred poems from Les fleurs du mal. Translated by C. F. MacIntyre. Berkeley and Los Angeles, University of California Press, 1947.

The Flowers of Evil. Selected and edited by Marthiel and Jackson Mathews. New York, New Directions, 1955.

The Flowers of Evil. Translated into English by Cyril Scott. London, Mathews, 1909.

Les fleurs du mal. The complete poems of Charles Baudelaire in English verse, translated by Lewis P. Shanks. London, Washburn, 1931.

Flowers of Evil. Translation by Geoffrey Wagner. Norfolk (Conn.), New Directions, 1949.

Intimate journals. Translated by Christopher Isherwood. Introduction by T. S. Eliot. London, Blackamore Press; New York, Random House, 1930.

Intimate journals. Translated by Christopher Isherwood. Introduction by W. H. Auden. Hollywood, M. Rodd, 1947.

Intimate journals. Translated by Christopher Isherwood. With an introduction by W. H. Auden. London, Methuen, 1949. (A revised edition of Isherwood's 1930 translation.)

The letters of Charles Baudelaire to his mother, 1833-1866. Translated by Arthur Symons. London, J. Rodker, 1927.

The mirror of art, critical studies. Translated and edited by Jonathan Mayne. London, Phaidon Press, 1955. (Phaidon Pocket Series.)

The mirror of Baudelaire. Edited by Charles Henri Ford, with a preface by Paul Eluard. Norfolk (Conn.), New Directions, 1942. (Poet of the Month, 1942, 12.)

My heart laid bare and other prose writings. Edited, with an introduction, by Peter Quennell. Translated by Norman Cameron. London, Weidenfeld & Nicholson, 1950; New York, Vanguard Press, 1951.

The painter of Victorian life. A study of Constantin Guys. Edited by Geoffrey Holme, with an introduction and a translation of Baudelaire's *Peintre de la vie moderne,* by P. G. Konady. London, Studio Ltd.,1930.

Paris spleen, 1869. Translated from the French by Louise Varèse. Norfolk (Conn.), New Directions, 1947.

The poems of Charles Baudelaire. Translated by F. P. Sturm. London, Walter Scott, 1906.

The poems and prose poems of Charles Baudelaire. With an introductory preface by James Huneker. New York, Brentano's, 1929.

Little poems in prose. Translated by A. Crowley. Illustrated by J. Bosschère. New York, Random House, 1928.

Poems in prose from Charles Baudelaire. Translated by Arthur Symons. Portland (Me.), T. B. Mosher, 1909.

Twenty prose poems of Baudelaire. Translated with an introduction by Michael Hamburger. London, Editions Poetry, 1946.

Selected poems. With translations by Geoffrey Wagner, and an introduction by Enid Starkie. London, Falcon Press, 1946.

Selected critical studies. Edited, with an introduction, by D. Parmée. Cambridge (England), Cambridge University Press, 1949.

Selections from Baudelaire's writings, prose and verse. Translated, with biographical and critical essay, by Grace King. New York, Knickerbocker Press, 1917. (The Warner Library of the World's Best Literature.)

READINGS:

Balakian, Anna. *Literary origins of surrealism, a new mysticism in French poetry.* New York, King's Crown Press, 1947. (Includes study of Baudelaire's influence on French surrealism.)

Bandy, William Thomas. *Baudelaire judged by his contemporaries (1845-1867).* New York, Columbia University Press, 1933. Another edition: Nashville, 1933 (George Peabody College for Teachers. Contributions to Education, 124.)

Bennett, Joseph D. *Baudelaire, a criticism.* Princeton, (N.J.), Princeton University Press, 1944.

Bowie, Theodore. *Baudelaire and the graphic arts.* Bloomington (Ind.), Indiana University, 1957. (Publication of the Department of Fine Arts, Indiana University.)

Carrère, Jean. *Regeneration in the great French masters.* New York, Brentano's, 1922. (Translation by Joseph McCable of Carrère's *Les mauvais maîtres.* Includes chapter on Baudelaire.)

The centennial celebration of Baudelaire's Les fleurs du mal. Austin (Tex.), University of Texas Press, 1958.

Chisholm, Alan Rowland. *Towards* Hérodiade, *a literary genealogy.* Melbourne, Melbourne University Press, in association with Oxford University Press, 1934. (Includes chapter on "Baudelaire and the doctrine of consequences."

————. "Baudelaire: the duality of the *Fleurs du mal*" in *French Quarterly* (Manchester, Eng.), v. 14 (1932), pp. 148-162.

Clapton, George Thomas. *Baudelaire and De Quincey.* Paris, Les Belles Lettres, 1931. (Etudes Françaises, 26.)

————. *Baudelaire, the tragic sophist.* Edinburgh, Oliver and Boyd, 1934.

189

————. "Carlyle and some early English critics of Baudelaire"· in *A miscellany of studies in Romance languages and literatures,* presented to Leon E. Kastner, pp. 128-146. Cambridge (Eng.), Cambridge University Press, 1932.

Eliot, T. S. *From Poe to Valéry.* New York, Harcourt, Brace, 1948.

————. "Baudelaire in our time"; in his *For Lancelot Andrews: essay on style and order,* pp. 86-99. London, Faber and Gwyer, 1928.

Fondane, Benjamin. "Baudelaire and the experience of the abyss"; translated by Lionel Abel in *Partisan Review* (New York), v. 10 (1943), pp. 410-420.

Fowlie, Wallace. "Baudelaire today"; in *Poetry* (Chicago), v. 82 (May, 1953), pp. 86-95.

————. *Clowns and angels; studies in modern French literature.* New York, Sheed and Ward, 1943. (Includes chapter on "Charles Baudelaire: the experience of religious heroism")

Gautier, Théophile. *Charles Baudelaire.* Translated into English by Guy Thorne. London, Greening, 1915. (Includes selections from Baudelaire's poems, prose, and letters.)

Gilman, Margaret. *Baudelaire the critic.* New York, Columbia University Press, 1943. (Includes notes, pp. 227-250; bibliography, pp. 251-255.)

Joost, N. "Poe as patron saint"; in *Poetry* (Chicago), v. 81 (January, 1953), pp. 247-251.

Jones, Percy Mansell. *Baudelaire.* New Haven (Conn.), Yale University Press, 1952. (Studies in European Literature and Thought.)

Laforgue, René. *The defeat of Baudelaire; a psychoanalytic study.* Translated from the French by Herbert Agar. London, L. and V. Woolf, 1932. (International Psycho-analytic Library, 21.) (Translation of Laforgue's *L'échec de Baudelaire.* Includes bibliography, and many poems with literal translations.)

Legge, James. *Chanticleer, a study of the French muse.* London, J. M. Dent, 1935. (Chapter VIII: "New departures: Baudelaire, the Parnassians, symbolism.")

Loving, Pierre. *Gardener of evil, a portrait of Baudelaire and his times.* New York, Brewer and Warren, 1931.

Mary Alphonsus [*mother*]: *The influence of Joseph de Maistre on Baudelaire.* Bryn Mawr (Pa.), n. p., 1943. (Doctoral thesis. Includes bibliography.)

Miller, L. Gardner. "Gustave Flaubert and Charles Baudelaire — their correspondence" in *Publications of the Modern Language Association of America,* v. 49 (1934), pp. 630-644.

Morgan, Edwin. *Flower of evil, a life of Charles Baudelaire.* New York, Sheed and Ward, 1943.

Porché, François. *Charles Baudelaire.* Translated by John Mavin. London, Wishart; New York, H. Liveright, 1928.

Quennell, Peter. *Baudelaire and the symbolists.* London, Chatto and Windus, 1929.

Raymond, Marcel. *From Baudelaire to surrealism.* Preface by Motherwell. Introduction by Harold Rosenberg. Bibliography by Bernard Karpel. New York, Wittenborn, Schultz, 1950. (Document of Modern Art, 10. Includes exhaustive bibliography, in French and English, pp. 365-428. On Baudelaire, see bibliography, pp. 390-393, and Raymond's introduction, pp. 5-40.)

Rhodes, Solomon A. *The cult of beauty in Charles Baudelaire.* 2 vols. New York, Institute of French Studies, Columbia University, 1929. (Doctoral dissertation. Bibliography, pp. 588-617, includes chronological list of Baudelaire's editions [1842-1928] and list of studies on Baudelaire [1855-1928].)

Sartre, Jean-Paul. *Baudelaire.* Translated from the French by Martin Turnell. Norfolk (Conn.), J. Laughlin, 1950. (Direction, 17.)

Schenck, Eunice Morgan and M. Gilman. "'Le voyage' and 'L'albatros'": the first text; in *Romanic Review* (N. Y.), v. 29 (1938), pp. 262-277.

Shanks, Lewis P. *Baudelaire, flesh and spirit.* Boston, Little, Brown, 1930.

Starkie, Enid M. *Baudelaire.* London, V. Gollancz; New York, G. P. Putnam Sons, 1933. Revised edition: New York, New Directions, 1958.

Symons, Arthur. *Charles Baudelaire, a study.* London, E. Mathews, 1920.

Turnell, Martin. *Baudelaire, a study of his poetry.* London, H. Hamilton, 1953; New York, New Directions, 1954.

Turquet-Milnes, Gladys R. *The influence of Baudelaire in France and England.* London, Constable, 1913.

Valéry, Paul. "The position of Baudelaire"; in his *Variety* (second series), pp. 71-98. Translated from the French by William Aspenwall Bradley. New York, Harcourt, Brace, 1938.

Vandérem, Ferdinand. "Baudelaire"; in *Bibliographie de la France. Supplément.* Paris, November 9, 1923, pp. 227-246.

Wright, Margaret Gilmore. *The role of the auditive sense in Baudelaire's works.* Philadelphia, University of Pennsylvania, 1929. (Doctoral thesis.)

(BIBLIOGRAPHY ESTABLISHED BY HELEN R. LANE.)

Dirt farming aint what it used to be — but then, it never was.

ACKNOWLEDGMENTS

The photographs of Baudelaire reproduced on pages 9, 115, 124 of this volume are from plates by Nadar; the portrait of Poulet-Malassis (p. 179) is also by Nadar.

The Baudelaire: Self-Portrait on page 4 is a drawing in ink and red crayon — dating, according to Jacques Crépet, from 1860.

The Baudelaire at the Age of Twenty on page 21 is a lead-pencil drawing (by an unknown artist) which once belonged to Catulle Mendès.

The title-page of the original edition of the *Fleurs du Mal* (p. 186) was photographed from a copy preserved in the Bibliothèque Jacques Doucet.

The illustrations reproduced on pages 53 and 180: Photos Giraudon; on pages 62 and 152: Photos Bulloz; on page 182: Archives Photographiques d'Art et d'Histoire.

The caricature of Balzac by Nadar (p. 160) and all other reproductions of works by Nadar are by courtesy of the Photographic Archives of Monuments Historiques.

The seven poems translated by C. F. MacIntyre are from *"One Hundred Poems from Les Fleurs du Mal,"* University of California Press, Berkeley and Los Angeles; reprinted by permission.